LADY WASHINGTON:

Age of Exploration Merchant Vessel

By Alexa Chipman

Imagination Lane

TABLE OF CONTENTS

1   Maritime Colonial America

8   The Northwest Expedition

16   To Cape Horn

26   The Southwest Coast

32   California & Oregon

45   The Northwest coast

61   A New Season

83   Kendrick Takes Command

92   China & Japan

100   Bold Northwestman

108   Macao & Hawaii

113   The Death of Kendrick

117   Final Years

129   Works Cited

In Memory of Charles Worsley

Special Thanks to:
Grays Harbor Historical Seaport

Imagination Lane
United States of America

Lady Washington:
Age of Exploration Merchant Vessel

ISBN 145384208X
EAN-13 9781453842089
United States—History—Revolutionary Period, Maritime

1: Maritime Colonial America

In the late eighteenth century, unrest was brewing in Colonial America. To the frustration of the British Parliament and those in authority, records from the colonies were chaotic at best. Ships were being constructed illegally, then given identical names and papers in order to evade payment of duties. Most of the paperwork flowing through ports was of questionable validity; smuggling was openly practiced and even encouraged by fellow citizens. If this made it difficult to accurately track sailing vessels at the time, it is made doubly so over a century later when many of the records have been lost. Tracing back the precise origin of the sloop *Lady Washington* is therefore in the realm of guesswork, rather than an exact science. Even when documentation is found listing a vessel of about the correct tonnage called *Washington*, it does not necessarily mean it is the one which later became famous in the Northwest voyages.

There are various popular theories regarding the construction of *Lady Washington*, or *Washington* as she might have been called at first. Maritime tradition indicates her shipyard was on the North River, possibly at Briggs yard. Historians have carefully examined the records from Briggs and found nothing which matches the future sloop close enough, so the theory is unlikely. Considering references to Rhode Island and Massachusetts, it is safe to assume she was constructed somewhere in that vicinity during the 1760s or early 1770s.

As the American Revolution rumbled into being, *Lady Washington* was on the forefront as a privateer. There is some dissension regarding the validity of the first documented entry for the sloop, but the argument in its favor appears to be sound. The letters of marque list Sam Brown among the owners, and he was later a partner in the Northwest Expedition for which *Lady Washington* was chosen. Her tonnage is placed at "about seventy tons" (Naval 291) which is not far removed from references to her having about ninety. The August 24, 1776 letters of marque are for a Rhode Island sloop *Lady Washington* from Newport with James Godfrey as Commander. According to the listing, she was armed to the teeth with cannon and small arms for her crew.

The first officer, Henry Weedon, was transferring from the privateer *Diamond*, where he had been second officer under William Chace. An important privateer in his own right, Chace was a skilful and experienced commander. Weedon would have learned a great deal under his tutelage, and brought this knowledge to the *Lady*. It is probable the other officers were already veteran privateers, such as Daniel Sewat who is listed as second officer of the *Lady*. The master, Thomas Cotterel, had been on a schooner that was captured and had returned to Providence after a daring escape.

Forty-six year old Peleg Chapman, a landowner in Newport, was also an officer. We know almost nothing about the *Lady's* common sailors, save that there was a Seth Melville on board. Numbers for her crew vary between fifty and seventy. Due to the size of the vessel, I believe the smaller number to be the more practical.

By October 7, 1776, *Lady Washington* was already on the hunt, and the Newport Mercury newspaper reported she had taken a British prize ship to Massachusetts. A few months later, she had taken several British vessels and done quite a lot of damage, despite her small size. Privateering was "a kind of large-scale private war, driven as much by profit as by patriotism" (Meltzer 169). Cargo from the captured ships sold for staggering amounts, even by modern standards, and items such as molasses, wool, and sugar were in great demand. There is an amusing story of some women in Boston literally attacking a merchant believed to be hoarding coffee, "a hundred assembled...one of them seized him by the neck, and tossed him into the cart" (Meltzer 87). I guess some things don't change—people still crave their caffeine. Samuel Brown and the other owners turned a tidy profit during *Lady Washington*'s privateering days.

Due to the fact there are almost ten different privateers named *Lady Washington*, most of the records cannot be entirely relied upon. For example, Edgar S. Maclay suggested that the sloop *Lady Washington*, under Captain Joseph

3

Cunningham, was involved in a battle during June of 1776 near Boston. If that is true, she is either not the same sloop mentioned in the August letters of marque, or she was being re-commissioned on that date. Cunningham's privateer had some crewing troubles, for she is stated as having at one point "only seven men on board" (Miller 79). Another *Lady Washington* was sent out from Rhode Island on November 12, 1776 under commander Ishmael Hardy of Massachusetts, but Samuel Brown is not listed as the owner, nor are any others involved in the later Northwest Expedition, so this is probably not the correct vessel.

These alternate sloops had exciting adventures of their own. For example, under Captain Cunningham, there is a tale during the war when an American ship was in danger. The schooner *Franklin*, under Captain Mugford, had been attempting to evade the enemy by keeping close in to shore. Heavily armed longboats of British filled with soldiers were sent to take the *Franklin*, but her captain would have none of it. In a brilliant, though daring move, he cut the *Franklin's* anchor so the ship swung ready to let off a broadside of grapeshot at the oncoming attackers. The blast destroyed two of the boats of men, but British boarders began pouring over the sides. The American crew bravely hacked away in defense of their ship, but all hope seemed to be lost until night fell, and "a small privateer, *Lady Washington*, joined the fight, in the darkness confusing the British into thinking they were outnumbered and prompting their retreat" (Patton

45). It was too late for the captain of the besieged ship, but Mugford's final words have gone down in history as having been "don't give up the vessel, you will be able to beat them off" (Patton 45). Even though this is probably not our *Lady Washington*, the idea of her coming to the rescue in the nick of time is a fine and noble moment.

June 13, 1779, a privateer *Lady Washington* under Captain Greenway set off with the privateers *Baltimore Hero* and *Lively* near the Rappahannock river. Enemy sails bore down on them—two nimble British privateers had in tow several prize ships captured from the Americans. Though outnumbered, the dauntless crew of *Lady Washington,* with her companions, assailed their adversaries. A battle of several hours ensued, and more British ships, "two brigs and several schooners of their fleet" (Scharf 208) arrived to join the fight. Despite the odds, the Americans rescued one of the prize ships and fled up river past Point-no-Point. Even though her two companions suffered severe damage, that particular *Lady Washington* apparently came through with few casualties. Since the vessel is described as a brig, under a different captain, there is serious doubt as to whether she was our *Lady Washington*, yet it is an engaging tale of privateers during the war.

The sloop was likely re-commissioned into a Massachusetts privateer August 12, 1777. Samuel Brown continued as an owner, and the crew were mostly residents of Boston.

Six years later the war ended. *Lady Washington* continued under Brown's ownership, and he went into partnership with Captain Crowell Hatch of Cambridge, who became co-owner. We do not know her activities until 1787, though during that time she was converted back into a merchant vessel, and probably sailed along the New England coast.

There is a darker side to the *Lady*'s original owner, for Samuel Brown of Boston was implicated with the infamous William Vernon of the slave trade. The Brown family had "slaving activity...long suspected by historians" although "less active and successful in the slave trade than once supposed" (Rawley 326). He financed attempts to pass legislation bringing back the slave trade in Massachusetts, and was a "hot head opposed to efforts to suppress the human traffic" (Rawley 301).

The evidence does not indicate that Brown or his ships were directly involved in the slave trade—rather he was a common financial backer and insurer of the slavers. He was extremely clever in avoiding laws in place restricting this, and advised William Vernon's slave ship *Pacific* to put in at New York, where it was least likely to have any trouble. It is perhaps lucky that *Lady Washington* had been moved to Boston, for soon after the war her former harbours Newport and Providence returned to the forefront of colonial slaving, and she might have become involved in that heinous trafficking.

After many years at sea as a captain and shipmaster, Crowell Hatch settled down and became a shipowner. He married Hannah Boit, daughter of a West India merchant, and had several children. Through his connections with the prominent Boit family, as well as an instinctual business sense, he did quite well and was influential in assisting various relatives to find berths on ships as well as becoming co-owner of *Lady Washington* and other merchant vessels. While comfortable in his retirement, one has the impression that his heart was always upon the sea.

The newly freed colonies needed to re-organize after the war. American merchants and businessmen scrambled to regroup, and there were debts and property loss to be dealt with. Trade between the states was the first to recover, as merchants of the struggling nation still felt a camaraderie which had been formed during the war. They saw opportunities in international trade and pooled their resources to meet that goal. Though circumstances were still uncertain, many set out for Asia and the West Indies. At first, American ships were met with incredulity and distrust, but over time they were able to earn the respect of international trading ports. There had been several attempts at a voyage to China, with varying results. In 1787, the *Lady*'s owners Brown and Hatch were invited to a meeting of influential Boston merchants.

Boston was one of the main areas for post-colonial trade, and Joseph Barrell was among the wealthiest merchants in the fledgling nation. He had many projects, including "merchant ships...fishing craft, whalers, and coasters" (Scofield 38). Inspired by Captain Cook's voyage, Barrell had got it into his head to send an expedition to China. Without the internet and easy ways to purchase articles from around the world, the colonies had to be content with what came into their ports. As a result, tea, silks, and other exotic goods were in great demand. The same was true of China, for they were enamored of sea otter furs from the Northwest coast of what later became the United States. Captain Cook had first discovered the potential of the fur trade when his crew stopped in Hawaii and sold their own coats due to the balmy weather.

Cook's ship set out for the cold climate of the Northwest, and sailors were desperate for something warm to wear. They noticed the Native Americans had sea otter pelt cloaks, and after purchasing many of them, Cook's expedition voyaged on to Canton, where the pelts became an instant obsession with the Chinese. From then on, merchant ships sailed along the Northwest coast to trade for furs, went west to China to trade for tea and other goods, then returned to their home ports bringing profit and thrilling tales of exotic cultures.

The merchants of Boston were determined to break into the profitable fur trade. In their minds it was a simple matter of buying a few beads for the Native Americans and reaping rich Chinese goods as a result. After having spent several years in England, Dr. Thomas Bulfinch moved in near Joseph Barrell and brought new information about the British fur trade. Excitedly, the two men began to plan an American expedition to China.

It became clear that adding more partners would be prudent, so Samuel Brown and Crowell Hatch joined the group. Other members included John Darby, who was a ship owner and former shipmaster, young John Marsden, and John M. Pintard, a merchant from New York. There were many meetings of the Barrell expedition financiers, who pooled 49,000 dollars for the venture. Dr. Bulfinch stepped back and was replaced by his son Charles, who was an architect. Each share was 3,500 dollars, although Barrell held four of the fourteen shares. What pride those men must have had as they strutted through Bostonian parlours with stories of their expedition—they even commissioned medallions to commemorate the occasion in silver, pewter, and copper. No doubt Samuel Brown enthusiastically handed out the small, yet exquisite medallions which bore both his name and that of his vessel *Lady Washington*.

Whether Brown or Hatch suggested the *Lady* we do not know, but the sloop was chosen as part of the Northwest

Expedition. She was to be tender, a vessel capable of carrying excess cargo, to the flagship *Columbia Rediviva*. At that time it was usual to have a smaller ship in accompaniment, "in accordance with the plan outlined in Cook's account" (Howay vi) which makes sense, for the partners had carefully studied all of the records pertaining to Cook's voyages. The *Columbia* was constructed in an older style with a wide hull and seemed large and clumsy beside the *Lady*. She was of an awkward size that was slower and less maneuverable than the sloop, while still not being large enough to be of significant use in trade. This was confirmed later, when the commander of the expedition tired of the flagship and opted to sail on *Lady Washington* instead. Since the *Columbia* was also owned by Crowell Hatch, it seems most likely that he was the one who decided to use the two ships in company.

The partners carefully chose the officers of expedition, partly from recommendations and possibly due to a bit of bribery in some cases. Often officers were men that one or more of the financiers, or their acquaintances, had worked with previously, as was the case with John Kendrick, who became overall commander of the expedition. Robert Gray was chosen to command *Lady Washington*, and had a reputation as a steady, reliable sort of man. While this was mostly true, he also had a dream to become an explorer of unknown lands, and in a later voyage, struck out on his own to explore the mysteries of the Northwest coast. He is famous for having come across the Columbia River, and to this day the state of Washington has a harbour named for him. The *Lady*'s captain was born in 1755 at Tiverton, Rhode Island, on his father's farm. It is possible he had seen or even sailed on *Lady Washington* as a young man, back in the days when she was a sloop in Newport. Like the *Lady*, there is very little information about Gray's youth. Maritime tradition places him in the American Navy during the revolution, however almost no evidence of this has been recovered, so it is more likely that he served on a privateer. By 1792 Robert Gray lost an eye, and it is possible this happened during the war, but we cannot be certain. Though he was left in poverty toward the end of his life, Gray was extremely close to his wife and daughters, and cared a great deal about his family. In 1806, the explorer was put to rest—his contribution to history not recognized until after his demise.

Lady Washington's first officer was David Coolidge, also known as Davis. He got along well with some of the difficult personalities of the expedition, so it is safe to assume that he was an amiable sort of man. There are several instances in journals where he went ashore on recreational explorations with other officers—he was clearly esteemed and good company. Coolidge stayed on board the *Lady* for quite some time. He was an adept officer, and a natural with languages. Coolidge was requested for a brief cruise as interpreter to the Native Americans in Nootka sound on board the Spanish vessel *Santa Gertrudis la Magna*. There were about ten men on board, twelve counting the captain and his servant. We have evidence of a gunner on later voyages, although the sloop did not have many cannon to begin with when she set out from Boston—maritime author Colonel Charles Parkin believed she had only one or two six pounders and four swivel guns.

It is difficult to know the exact specifications of the *Lady* herself at the time of the expedition, for we have only a few passing references by other ship captains and a rough sketch to go by. Tradition places her as a ninety ton sloop, and Colonel Parkin stated that, if so, "her other measurements, according to the formula then in use, should be approximately: length 64'-00"; breadth 20'-06"; depth 8' " (95). This is less than the size of a tennis court, and once you add in all the men, animals, supplies, rigging, and cargo it makes for a very tight space indeed.

The 1787 journal sketch of *Lady Washington* gives her a mainmast and extra long jib. According to the medallion struck in the same year depicting the sloop under full sail, she had a square topsail on her mast above the mainsail and three headsails. What colors she was painted remain a mystery, but we do know her hull just above the waterline was white, with three main stripes of colour above that. Based on the black and white sketch, it is probable that the next line above white was either red or blue since it is shown as a darker line. Above that is a light gray possibly depicting a yellow, then a dark line which could be red or blue. Both the replica and later maritime paintings chose a yellow and blue scheme for the *Lady*, since that was typical of the era of her construction. The key with a merchant vessel was to keep the hull bright and appealing so that traders and Native Americans could easily locate the sloop.

The *Lady* had charts of as much of the Pacific Ocean as was available at the time. There were charts of the Northwest coast from Cook's voyages that were, no doubt, on board. Several Spanish maps had been translated by 1775 and examples of them have been recorded as being standard on American and British fur trade vessels. William Faden had a set of updated charts of the areas covered by Cook published in 1785, and the *Lady* also probably had them. James Hanna and James Strange were on the Northwest coast fur trading in 1785-6, though their charts were not officially published until 1789. It is still possible that one of the Barrell expedition found a way to see the charts pre-publication, though they did not depict much that was not present in the maps of Captain Cook.

Because of her smaller size, *Lady Washington* did not anchor right away with the flagship *Columbia Rediviva*, since it would take less time to equip the sloop for sea. On Friday, September 28, 1787 she slipped in beside the larger ship and dropped anchor near Castle Island in the President Roads, just outside the inner harbour. While Castle Island is now connected with the mainland, in *Lady Washington's* time it was well out from shore, in between Pleasure Bay, Spectacle Island, and Thompson Island. A fort stood on the small piece of land, know as "Castle William", with basic fortifications and a group of buildings. Less than two days after dropping anchor there, the sloop sailed, so it is possible that some supplies had already been brought on board prior to her arrival.

There was cargo to help the sloop herself—such as lanterns, bolts, oil, rigging, files, twine, jacks, canvas, and spare sails, as well as powder, shot, and a small arms chest in case of trouble. The financiers added trade items they thought Native Americans would be interested in, though it is amusing to read the list—eighteen rat traps, 180 necklaces, nineteen egg slicers, 449 mirrors, seventy-eight snuff bottles, 273 Jews' harps, 168 earrings, and ninety-two pounds of beads. The population along the coast was as dubious about the items as we are today, and that bit of cargo was basically useless. Fortunately, some unworked metals were also put on board, which the crew put to use in trading during the voyage.

Lady Washington was also supplied with ship's biscuit, salted meat, water, and rum, as well some fresh provisions which would be used as long as they lasted, and of course at every available opportunity during the voyage, her crew went hunting, or at least shot anything edible that came in range of the sloop.

Though some of the financiers were quite busy and had multiple trade projects, they probably stopped by at least once to see how work was getting on before the ships sailed. It is difficult for us to comprehend how exciting it was to have a ship going to the other side of the world—we can hop on a plane any time we like and be there in hours or have a video conference between China and the United States without any trouble at all. They were facing months at sea in dangerous, almost unknown waters, venturing to places few Americans had ever been. Most of their knowledge came from rumour and somewhat imaginative narratives.

3: To Cape Horn

Most of the officers came aboard *Lady Washington* on Saturday, September 29 with their baggage. The common sailors were put to work clearing the deck of any last minute stores and completing final preparations. That night was party time—lasting through into morning light. The sloop was full of friends, families, well wishers, and most of the financiers having a last look at their investment. On Sunday morning, the pilot came on board, along with more Bostonians who obviously considered a joy ride on the sloop a better time than sitting through a three hour sermon. Imagine getting to tell everyone you were on board when the Barrell expedition set out for China! The first few days were more like a floating celebration than a serious voyage.

Lady Washington leisurely made her way across the harbour to Nantasket Roads where she anchored again for a night of gaiety. According to a journal, "the evening was spent in mirth and glee the highest flow of spirits animating the whole company. Jovial songs...the most tender expressions of friendship...wishes for our prosperity resounded from every tongue," (Voyages 4). Despite the late night, *Lady Washington* up anchored and sailed before sunrise the next morning and on October 1, 1787 left Boston forever. There was a good wind for the next few weeks, and the sloop's crew settled into their routine. Captain Gray was able to observe how well the *Lady* sailed, and the dependability of his officers. They passed many other brigs and schooners, since they were still in a heavy shipping area.

Lady Washington paused for a week at the Isle of May, also called Maio, one of the southern Cape Verde islands in the north Atlantic ocean. The main export of the island was salt, and it was small, rocky, and sandy without much fresh water. The main reason for the halt was to add to the provisions— particularly in the form of livestock. Even though the sloop did not have much room, she needed a manger. The larger ship of the expedition took on forty goats, two bulls, a cow, three hogs, and three sheep. The *Lady* had a goat named Nancy, which Captain Gray was fond of, so the sloop probably had on board at least a hog, some goats, chickens, and possibly a sheep as well.

On the sixteenth of October, *Lady Washington* up anchored for St. Jago, another island of Cape Verde. The population of St. Jago was friendly and well-ordered. The captain was so impressed that he brought one of the native lads along. Marcus Lopius came aboard as Robert Gray's servant—the duties were fairly similar to a servant on shore, and he was most definitely not a slave, though Lopius had a dark complexion typical of the natives. He must have been adventurous to ship out for parts unknown as a young man, and Gray seemed to think him a capable worker to bring him along to the Northwest coast. Being the captain's servant was a difficult life, because the crew looked down on him, and thus Lopius had no companions to talk and laugh with during the long voyage. Even the sloop's officers had each other, but Lopius was on his own.

If the lad expected to head out to sea right away, he was disappointed. To Captain Gray's surprise, the head of the expedition decided to completely reorder the hold of his ship—an undertaking which ended up taking over a month. For some reason, the *Columbia's* hold had been incorrectly stowed in Boston, and goods were on top of the spare water casks, as well as other serious mistakes which needed rectifying. The animals on board the *Lady* were put back on shore temporarily, and tents were set up with the permission of the island's governor. Everyone had to sit and wait while Captain Kendrick of the *Columbia* worked hard to overhaul his ship properly. Without much to do, and frustrated that they were laid up, the crews took to quarrelling.

On the evening of November 7, 1787, the *Lady's* crew heard shouting on the other ship, and next thing they knew, Simeon Woodruff, first officer of *Columbia*, came over in a boat and clambered aboard *Lady Washington* fuming with anger. He had never got on well with his captain, and had been chosen by the financiers for the fact he had been part of Cook's expedition, rather than as a friend of Kendrick. It came to a head in a furious exchange ending in his being removed or resigning as first mate—opinions of historians differ as to that matter. The excitement was not over for the night, because after a few hours another boat came alongside the *Lady*, with Richard Howe on board.

Mr. Howe was the supercargo of the flagship, and also assisted as captain's clerk upon occasion. He had some papers for Woodruff to sign, but the gentleman was hardly in the mood, and they were apparently rather rudely worded. Another argument took place with Howe, who went back to the *Columbia* in a huff with the unsigned papers. Just when Captain Gray was hoping the matter had come to a close for the evening, along came the creak and splash of oars as young Robert Haswell, an officer on *Columbia*, arrived to convey the order that Woodruff and his baggage were to be sent back with all possible speed. Probably glad to be rid of the disturbance, Gray complied, and Mr. Woodruff was sent with Haswell. The next day, the former first officer was taken ashore where he found a ship to convey him back home.

At long last, on the twenty-first of December, *Lady Washington* sailed away from the Cape Verde islands. The weather held, although there were often brief showers of rain. Some of the men fished to augment the food supply, and tempers began to improve on the sloop. Unfortunately, relations on the flagship were still strained, and when Captain Gray and Mr. Coolidge the first mate went for what should have been a calm dinner on the other ship, it did not end well. The captain of *Columbia*, Kendrick, ordered his men aft, and sent Robert Haswell to see to it. Gray must have inwardly groaned when sounds came of a scuffle and blows being struck. He and Coolidge went with the other officers to see what the matter was and found a sailor swearing and covered with blood, an equally irate twenty-year-old Haswell, and first mate Ingraham shouting them both down.

As is usual in such situations, everyone had a different story. The sailor, John Liscomb, claimed the young officer had dragged him by the collar, then assaulted him for no reason. Haswell said that Liscomb had refused to obey orders and used such terrible language that there was no choice but to strike him. The first mate of Columbia, though not present at the incident, was moved by the poor sailor who was bleeding and took sides against the second mate. In the heat of the moment, Kendrick used all the foul repertoire at his command to berate Haswell, who described it as, "language to horrid to be repeated," (Voyages 12) and began landing angry blows with his fist on the young man, who grabbed the captain's arm and forced him to stop.

Kendrick stepped aside and bellowed that if he ever saw Haswell on the quarter deck again he'd blow his brains out with a pistol. Turning to the horrified officers present, the captain shouted that if anyone saw Haswell disobeying that order they were to knock him over the head. The young officer was sent to clear out his cabin and a bewildered Mr. Howe ordered to occupy it instead. The disrated Haswell stormed off to pack his baggage and no doubt took time to enter some choice complaints about Kendrick in his journal. A shocked Captain Gray and Coolidge returned to the *Lady*, no doubt glad their own sloop was better ordered than the flagship and grateful for some peace and quiet.

In February, Kendrick announced his intention not to try for Cape Horn during the winter, but rather to stay and wait for a better season. His reasoning was sound—the Cape was dangerous at the best of times, and many a fine ship had been lost in the dreadful storms. With two older and relatively small ships, Kendrick was not certain they would make it round alive. When he expressed this to the officers and Captain Gray of *Lady Washington*, who were tired of sitting around, they, "immediately expressed their disgust at the very idea," (Voyages 14). It was their opinion that waiting on a remote bit of land would mean as much hardship as an attempt at the Cape would. Captain Gray was especially adamant, and said that he, "would try it in the sloop and had not the least doubt of succeeding," (Voyages 15). After Gray's impassioned speech that his *Lady Washington* would easily make the passage, Kendrick relented. Whether he wanted to avoid open conflict, or felt outdone by Gray's confidence in the *Lady* we do not know, but both vessels set out for Cape Horn.

It came as no surprise when, on March 28, 1788, Robert Haswell came aboard *Lady Washington* as her new second officer. The young man had requested a transfer right after the incident in December, but for some reason his captain kept him on board *Columbia* for three months. Kendrick did give a formal apology, but it had to be difficult working next to each other for that long after such a violent falling out. It was a poor time of the year to be setting out for Cape Horn, and Haswell noted some misgivings as he came aboard *Lady Washington*, "we were launching forward in a sloop scarcely ninety tons to make a passage at the same season of the year when Lord Anson in one of the finest ships in the British Navy met with almost insurmountable difficulties" (Voyages 18). If you are wondering why an American officer would be mentioning a Royal Navy ship with ease and even admiration, it can be explained by knowing more of Haswell.

Robert Haswell was born November 24, 1767 in Hull, Massachusetts. His father was a lieutenant in the Royal Navy, and his family had a long tradition of loyalty to the crown. He was still a child during the revolution, and his family actively supported the king and even harboured a wounded Royal Marine after the Battle of Boston Light in 1775. The Haswells were harshly treated by rebel colonials and his family eventually fled to Hull in Yorkshire, England where their relatives were. Robert Haswell decided not to join the British Navy, but did have solid sea experience before 1787 since he was placed as third mate on the flagship. It is possible his father might have financially arranged for the appointment, for he came with Robert to sell off their old property in Hull while the expedition was formed, and

Haswell opened his journal with "early in the fitting of the *Columbia* for a voyage round the world, I was employed as third officer" (Voyages 3). However frustrated he was with Kendrick, from the young man's journals it is plain that he wanted to go on that "voyage round the world" and part of the reason for his spats with the captain might have been the fact that Kendrick was a passionate revolutionary and did not appreciate having a Tory officer.

Rough seas began in mid-March of 1788, and Haswell described how, "these damps and the sprays continually flying over us rendered our duty prodigious hard and fatiguing... the clothes of all our people have been wet," (Voyages 19). If you have ever been caught out in the rain and had to walk a considerable distance, you will know how uncomfortable being cold and wet through can be. Clothes chafe even with simple movements, and trying to sail a ship in that sort of condition for days on end must have been miserable. The crew began seeing large islands of ice as the weather grew continuously colder. At last the sun came out, glistening on the sparkling blocks of ice, but it was only a momentary gleam, "the weather was very changeable from clear and pleasant to snow, hail, rain and sleet and from that to clear in the space of half an hour," (Voyages 20). Imagine standing on deck enjoying a relatively pleasant day when clouds suddenly race in and a severe hailstorm begins almost out of nowhere. It is easier to deal with inclement weather when it is expected, and such constant changes must have been beyond frustrating. Often the crew would find *Lady Washington* covered in a hard frost and their bedding frozen, due to the fact all the clothes and blankets had been soaked through with salt water from the rain and spray. Whenever they tried to properly dry anything in the sun, clouds would roll in and a new sheet of rain made it impossible. I must say that when I've been out camping and got soaked by an unexpected storm, the idea of warm clothes and blankets back in the tent made it all okay and even enjoyable—coming off watch to more wet and cold must have been depressing and difficult.

In the early darkness of the first of April, *Lady Washington* wore ship as the winds increased to gale force. When what could be seen of the sun rose in the morning, *Columbia* was nowhere in sight. There was no way to search for her in such heavy seas, and Captain Gray was more than happy to be shed of Kendrick, as he expressed in a letter to the financier Joseph Barrell, "I had the good luck to part company...in a severe gale and thick snow storm," (Voyages 122). They did not have much time to savour the parting, for Haswell describes how, "the wind blew heavy a perfect hurricane accompanied with rain, hail, snow and sleet with an intense frost...our sloop scudded exceeding well" (20 Voyages). There were waves higher than her mast rising up and plummeting down on all sides, snow whirled round biting into the crew's faces and skin as a wind blew so hard little could be done but stagger against it. There was a slight lull during the night, but at four o'clock in the morning of April second, a sudden violent wind squall took away *Lady Washington's* jib stay. The weather did not relent, and the sailors were exhausted and freezing. Two men had to go out and take down the old jib stay, and the officers were the only ones fit to make the attempt. Haswell and Coolidge staggered forward into whirling wind and icy blasts. With great difficulty they managed to haul in the old jib stay just as a fresh hailstorm began—pelting them with freezing hard balls of ice flung like bullets in the heavy wind. The weather was so harsh that it was not until the next day that they tried to fit a temporary stay. By the evening of April third, *Lady Washington* finally began limping on ahead away from the Horn.

Violent storms continued for weeks as *Lady Washington* made steady progress. Just when the crew of the sloop began to hope they would be lucky enough to escape unscathed, a worse squall suddenly blew up on the thirteenth at four o'clock in the afternoon. There came a loud rending tear as their sturdy mainsail, which had held on through terrible gales. It split badly and began flapping uselessly in the wind. The only replacement sail on board was made of old canvas and showed its wear. With no choice, they put it to use and the storm mercifully abated. The next day, on Monday, the hands were put feverishly to work mending the sail in more pleasant weather. Encouraged, Haswell wrote that he "began to experience that beautiful serenity this ocean is celebrated for," (Voyages 21). With a calm sea for the first time in weeks, the crew began to feel that the worst was over. Fingers began to thaw out, clothes dried, and spirits rose. *Lady Washington* sailed on and was greeted by dolphins, jellyfish, and flying fish frolicking about the sloop. The hardship of the Horn was over—they were the first vessel under an American flag to have braved the passage and had come successfully to the west coast of the continent.

Lady Washington was in dire need of a re-supply—particularly water and timber. The nearest convenient place was Masafuera, and Captain Gray began making his way to it. Masafuera is an island off the coast of Chile and almost straight out from Santiago. It is in a cluster of islands near the famous Robinson Crusoe, Santa Clara, and Alejandra Selkirk. The island is only about six by four miles, and is rocky and mountainous. Due to the wind being a bit strong, *Lady Washington* hove to and waited for morning before standing in to shore. In bright sunshine at ten o'clock on Wednesday, April 22, 1788, the longboat was sent out under the command of Coolidge—Captain Gray probably considered the mission important enough to send the first officer, or he was not yet certain whether Haswell was trustworthy enough. The surf was rough and there was a constant white spray tossed up by treacherous underwater rocks ringing the island. From the evidence of modern satellite images and photographs of the island, most of it would have been quite daunting to row past. Who would want to risk their life making a landing through surf filled with rows of jagged rocks when there were other islands near at hand?

Coolidge returned and made it quite clear that landing would be madness and there was no way the island of Masafuera could be used. Gray sadly gave the order to sail on, and did not question the officer's judgement—no doubt the captain could see the unfavorable coastline from where the *Lady* lay offshore. It was difficult to leave, because they could clearly see streams of water pouring down forested hills to the shore.

Haswell commented that the island itself had everything the *Lady* needed, but anyone who attempted to avail themselves of it would be a "highly imprudent" (Voyages 23) navigator.

Captain Gray had to make a difficult decision—should he go to the nearest well stocked Spanish port and risk losing the ship, or try to find an unoccupied island to collect water on. His concern was not ill-founded, for when the Spanish heard about *Lady Washington* and *Columbia* near their southern coast, they were given orders to capture the ships. Even as she sailed past San Francisco, the sloop was in danger from the commandant there. In the end, due to their small size and lack of serious cannon on board, Gray decided the only prudent course of action was to land on one of the Ambrose Islands. This may seem logical, but due to faulty charts, an earlier ship under Captain Carteret who searched for the islands never found them.

It speaks much of the fear which Gray had of the *Lady* falling into Spanish hands that he decided to attempt finding islands that others had failed to locate in an area of the sea he had never been in before. When news of the decision came to the crew, no doubt they were a bit worried. It would be easy to sail right past the Ambrose Islands, and they lay well up the coast. In anticipation, Captain Gray ordered the allowance of water lowered to two quarts a day and put the men to work beginning as many repairs as possible while still at sea.

In less than a week, on Saturday, May 3 at ten o'clock in the morning, land was sighted. Every bit of canvas was packed out in the excitement, but it took another two days to be near enough to send a boat ashore. The Ambrose Islands are now known as the Desventuradas Islands, with San Félix slightly north of San Ambrosio. They are in between Antofagasta and Huasco in Chile, only out in the sea. San Ambrosio is about three miles by one mile—even smaller than Masafuera. It is described in several journals as being extremely volcanic and uninviting. Coolidge took the boat out again, and the *Lady* herself sailed all the way round the island. The boat crew managed to land, but could not see any fresh water. Coolidge decided to try climbing higher to view the land, but found that the rocks were too unstable and dangerous. Every time he and the sailors tried to climb, the cliff would give way. In the end, they decided it was not worth risking their neck for. Instead, the men shot some seals that were lounging about down at the shore, and extracted oil from them.

Coolidge returned to the sloop with a negative report, and, as Captain Gray had been unable to see evidence of fresh water during his sail round San Ambrosio, he decided to press on, assuming that the nearby San Félix would not have water either. A few members of the crew wanted to give the other island a try, including Haswell, but Gray did not want to waste more time and some historians have argued he also did not want to run the risk of Kendrick overtaking them in the *Columbia*.

Part of the reason the men grumbled about the decision to sail on, ignoring the other island, is that water was beginning to run short. It had been some time since the last supply, and they were not able to simply turn on a faucet or run out to a well—they only had increasingly putrid supplies in fewer and fewer barrels. Just as it was becoming nearly unbearable, there was a long rainstorm, and the crew managed to store a decent amount of rainwater which kept them going. Fishing was very popular on board, and they caught turtles, fish, and dolphins with ease. No matter how many turtles could be consumed, it did not help with the problem of scurvy. One by one, the crew of *Lady Washington* fell victim to that dreaded disease which is caused by a lack of Vitamin C. Though the nature of scurvy was still unclear during the eighteenth century, it was known that fresh greens and fruit seemed to cure it. Some sailors believed merely standing on shore would fix the problem.

Poor young Marcus Lopius, the captain's servant, might never have seen the effects of scurvy before and would have been quite horrified as his comrades' gums swelled, legs stiffened, and teeth fell out. Gray knew time was short for his crew, and the need to find a landing place swiftly became all the more urgent. Interestingly, in a similar situation on a British naval warship, the commander was a botanist. When his crew developed scurvy, he gave up his prize collection of plants to make a salad for the crew, and thus saved their lives. On board *Lady Washington*, the wind held and whales began appearing near the sloop—plunging in and out of the waves and blowing puffs into the air. Haswell describes, "several whales of a considerable size, many seals were playing round us" (Voyages 28).

For the first time in months, land was sighted—on Saturday, August 2, 1788, the crew saw a hazy outline of what they called the coast of New Albion, which is one of the ancient names for the island of Britain, and often used in connection with King Arthur. The general area of the Oregon Coast has been called by that name from the first charts, and New Albion signified that the shore was like a new ancient Britain—unspoiled and beautiful. Her latitude put the *Lady* parallel with what is now Six Rivers National Forest in California near White Rock. On the fourth, the day began quite foggy, but a wind picked up and in the late morning they saw their first Native Americans. A friendly local group were curious about the lovely little sloop sailing along their coast and came paddling out with, "very expressive signs of friendship," (Voyages 29). Their wooden canoe was highly decorated in bright colours. The natives wore deerskins and beads and smiled at the newcomers—they were as interested in *Lady Washington* as the crew were of them.

Officers and hands alike crowded up to the rail to see the canoe. Captain Gray, eager to establish friendly relations, handed over presents and tried to speak with them. The natives were of the Yurok tribe—a kindly culture who were fond of boats and rivers. Gazing at the redwood clad shore, Haswell remarked that, "the country from whence these people came to me appeared the most pleasant I had ever

seen" (Voyages 30). The visit was cut short by another gale
approaching, and the *Lady* had to stand off shore for safety.

The next day, *Lady Washington* made good time, sailing
past the rest of northern California and into Oregon near
Goat Island and across from Brookings. More natives came
paddling out in the next few days, waving items to trade
with. Since the wind was so fair, Captain Gray decided to
press on ahead, rather than stop to trade, and was followed
by many canoes. The beauty of the Oregon coast was not lost
on the crew of the *Lady*. Haswell described it as, "a delightful
country thickly inhabited and clothed with woods and
verdure with many charming streams of water gushing from
the valleys" (Voyages 31). They saw some Native American
villages and huts near the shore, and the reaction of the
inhabitants to the sloop was varied. Some were frightened
and ran for the cover of trees, while others were so fascinated
that they ran along the shore for miles to watch the sloop sail
gracefully past their coast.

On Thursday, August 7, Captain Gray chose to send the boat
out again. They were southeast of Cape Blanco in Oregon,
and there was a large deep bay with a small island running
along it. The boat crew sounded the channel, and signalled
that there was plenty of depth, but when the *Lady* followed,
it turned out that it was not an ideal navigation situation, so
she came about and went on north. They continued, sailing
dangerously close to shore, and Haswell spotted a wide inlet

where he thought a large river was. Based on the latitude given, it was most likely the Alsea or Yachats River. Gray did not think it worth stopping for, particularly since the natives had changed from being friendly and curious to gathering on the shore shouting and shaking their spears and weapons. They wore a sort of armour made of moose deer layered together and tanned, which could stop the penetration of arrows during a battle. Their bows were of such a length as to impress the crew of the *Lady*. Sound carries well over water, and they were making what Haswell called, "horrible cries" (Voyages 32) and behaving with extreme hostility. The natives were not all unfriendly, for when the sloop wore ship and stood in to shore, a small canoe came cautiously over, crafted with a different design from those of the Yurok. They did not come too close to the *Lady*, and managed to convey through hand gestures that they had fish and fresh water on shore. Captain Gray tried to reply in a similar pantomime that they were only interested in sea otter skins. The natives paddled round the *Lady*, examining her closely, and Gray gave them presents which they seemed happy to receive before going back to shore.

On the tenth, Coolidge took the boat out to search for a safe landing place, and while he was gone more canoes came up to the *Lady*. One of them had the natives from the day before on board who had brought sea otter skins which they waved at the sloop. Though the natives were there for trade, they did not completely trust the crew of *Lady Washington* any more than the crew entirely trusted the natives. As a precaution, they were armed with bows and arrows as well as spears and knives. Captain Gray decided the possibility of otter skins was worth the risk of allowing one of them on board, but insisted the native leave his weapons. For some reason, Gray decided not to purchase the skins, but was cordial to the guest, who departed promising to spread the word about *Lady Washington*'s interest in otter skins. The sloop continued up the coast, and Coolidge had a bit of luck with the longboat—he was able to find a landing near a deserted native encampment and brought back two loads of wood to the sloop.

On Wednesday the thirteenth, a long canoe with twelve Native Americans paddled up—the men seemed fascinated by the sloop and very curious, though they had nothing to trade with. Captain Gray thought it would be wise to invite their chief on board as a gesture of friendship. The elderly native was given a tour of the sloop, and was quite interested in what Gray showed him. After receiving a few gifts, the native canoe returned to shore.

The *Lady*'s small size and draft proved useful when a harbour was spotted protected by a bar. Captain Gray could not resist the opportunity to explore, and sent the boat into what is now known as Tillamook Bay near Garibaldi, Oregon on August 14, 1788. The boat took careful soundings of the best route for the sloop to follow, and discovered the channel was possible to navigate. Hearing the good news, Captain Gray ordered the *Lady* in, and she sailed round the bar without any trouble into the protected bay. The Tillamook Native Americans were shocked to see the sloop—no such vessel had ever entered their harbour before, and naturally everyone who had a canoe put it into the water to have a closer look. They were a generally peaceful people who enjoyed watercrafts and had a rich cultural tradition. Captain Gray gave out many trinkets, and as the crew were in desperate need of fresh food to stave off scurvy, he also accepted large quantities of edible berries which were brought to the sloop. The people suffering from the disease quickly began eating as many as possible, and the offerings of the Tillamook natives may have saved their lives.

By the evening of the fifteenth, Gray succeeded in assuring the natives that he was safe and friendly. Sea otter furs were brought for him to examine, and the captain decided it was high time the *Lady* began the work she had been sent to do. He purchased several quality skins for knives and axes, though he realized for the first time how pitiful the trade items on board the *Lady* were. Most of the Tillamook natives were interested in copper, though they were very obliging to Captain Gray and were willing to compromise. It might have been due to the excitement of the sloop actually in their harbour, because usually natives along the coast had no interest in things like axes and knives. Confident in his purchases, Gray turned once more to his crew and the sloop—sending boats ashore for water and additional wood. This made him a bit nervous, since the fresh water supply was far from the protection of the *Lady*'s guns, and if the shore party ran into any trouble they would be on their own. The crew had no problems, and found the Tillamook friendly. Several natives gathered to watch the curious operation of filling water casks—even bringing fruit to the men at work.

By the next day, the sloop was completely surrounded with canoes that were filled with people shouting and waving items for sale—boiled and roasted crabs, salmon, and other fish, which some of the crew bought for buttons. If you think about it—buttons are rather difficult to make, especially the more ornate ones. The next time you put on a shirt take a close look at them—buttons really are quite exquisite to those who don't have any. Before you chortle at why the natives would sell crab for such items, think carefully—even today a decent set of buttons at a fabric store isn't cheap, whereas crabs were abundant in the area.

The canoe with the old chief who had come aboard before arrived with an escort of armed warriors and wanted to come aboard again, but Captain Gray didn't quite like the look of the group, and made it clear that he was only interested in trading for furs. Gray tried to be as polite as he could, and the chief was paddled back to shore. The bay was very calm, and the narrow entrance could only be safely used during

certain tides, so Gray had to wait for an opportune moment
to risk taking the *Lady* out again. He decided to send the
boat to gather as much food for the animals on board as
possible while in a good harbour. Faced with little to do but
wait, the officers petitioned to go ashore with the boat and
look around. Gray gave permission, so Coolidge and Haswell
clambered in, eager for some fun on an unexplored bit of
new land. Marcus Lopius watched the two young men head
off toward the native village with regret—Gray had ordered
him to help procure grasses and shrubs for the animals.
Hacking at bushes and weeds with a cutlass is not one of
the more interesting ways to spend a day, but he was a hard
worker. He slashed up enough greens to make a pile, then
stuck the cutlass into the sand, picked up the mound of sweet
smelling grass and dumped it in the boat.

After several trips, Marcus began to get careless about
keeping a watch on the cutlass, and as his aching arms
brought yet another load, he paused with his back to the
sword for a few seconds. That was all it took, for a curious
native pulled out the intriguing weapon. Marcus whirled
on him and the frightened man took off running—without
putting the cutlass back. Marcus knew how upset Captain
Gray would be about a native stealing the sword out from
under his nose, so he pursued the man, shouting for him
to drop it. Of course, the native couldn't understand what
Marcus was saying and kept running.

Haswell and Coolidge had been having a grand time—they visited several types of houses, and had a laugh about the strange foods that the natives kept offering. As Haswell remarked, "nothing we could stomach except the fruit," (Voyages 37). They walked by some warriors who were practicing with arrows and spears, and were impressed with their dexterity. They watched with amusement, and some consternation, as the Tillamook demonstrated their form of dance, then wandered along the pristine beach and began digging for shellfish. It is highly likely that Haswell had the idea to do so, since he'd spent his childhood in Cape Cod and would have dug clams along the beaches. As the young officers amused themselves, laughing and feeling at home for the first time in months, shouting was heard, then a shot rang out.

Wasting no time, Haswell sprinted toward where he had left the boat, furiously shouting at the man still holding a smoking gun. The second mate had left strict orders not to fire except in a dire emergency, and the sailor quickly explained what had happened with the cutlass, and that he had fired in an attempt to scare the native into dropping the stolen sword. Haswell turned to Coolidge in horror—they both knew that the Cape Verde lad was in danger. The natives would not understand, and would only see one of their own being chased down. Images of the skilled demonstrations of archery and spears came back to their minds, and the two officers raced off in the direction Marcus had taken, ordering the boat to row parallel with them ready for a swift retreat if necessary. As they reached the village, Coolidge spotted several important chiefs that he had exchanged gifts with. He paused and tried his best to explain the situation, begging for their help in bringing Marcus back unharmed. Perhaps they did not follow what Coolidge was trying to express, or they had other reasons for staying out of the conflict, but both chiefs refused to assist the chief mate. Looking carefully around, Haswell quietly pointed out to the first officer that all the natives in the village were carrying more arms than usual, and he had a bad feeling about the situation.

Marcus continued to pelt after the native, and in a brief spurt of extra speed, he tackled the man. Pulling him roughly up on his feet, the lad began yelling, "I caught the thief" as loud as he could. Round a thick grove of trees, Marcus spotted Haswell and Coolidge running up and joyfully shook the native again, shouting to them. How Captain Gray would be proud of him! Before the two officers could warn Marcus, he felt a stab of pain and gasped as several natives stabbed their spears and knives into him. He fell to his knees, crying out, and lost his grip on the native he had collared. Terrified and faint from the blood seeping out of his wounds, Marcus began stumbling his way toward Haswell and Coolidge. Before the officers could help him, expert native archers let off a volley into the lad's back. He collapsed, still trying to reach Coolidge, in a pool of his own blood. The two mates turned to leave, but found that natives from the village, gripping their weapons in grim determination, silently blocked the way back. The men of the *Lady* stepped forward, wanting to help Marcus, but were stopped by a flurry of arrows embedding into the ground in front of them. Haswell and Coolidge ducked as deadly feather shafts flew by. Searching for a break in the lines of Tillamook, the officers of *Lady Washington* made a dash for it as spears and arrows whizzed past—they had no time to go back for Marcus. The officers did not want to have to begin shooting the natives, but a courageous archer ran up for a point blank attempt at them, and Haswell had to take him out with a pistol. They continued to shoot natives who came too close.

The men waiting at the boat saw Coolidge dashing toward the shore shouting to give covering fire. He was followed by Haswell and a couple of men from the *Lady* who raced into the water, but were not quick enough. Slowed by having to wade through the bay, the crew became perfect targets for the natives. Coolidge was wounded, but staggered on, Haswell's hand ripped open as an arrow grazed past, and mere feet from the boat, waist high in the bay, one of the men fell into the water with a shaft buried deep into his body. Another member of the crew swam to him, hauled him into the boat, and they rowed back to the *Lady* with all possible speed. Before the sloop could be reached, canoes were launched, moving swiftly to cut the longboat off from the sloop. Haswell and

Coolidge, with those who were still able, kept up a constant fire from the boat, which kept them at bay.

Captain Gray watched as the boat approached under duress, with several men clearly wounded. He ordered the swivel guns loaded, and as soon as his men were safely on board, the guns echoed across the bay, frightening off canoes of natives. Within minutes, the harbor was flat and calm—eerily calm, with no sign of a native in sight. The badly injured crewman was unconscious for hours from loss of blood, but made it through after the arrow was carefully removed and wound staunched. That night the *Lady* rocked in fitful watch, her crew listening to war whoops round fires on shore. Haswell, his hand bandaged and still stinging with pain, furiously recommended that they attack the natives and have revenge for the slaughter of Marcus. Captain Gray showed his quality and refused to attack them— he chose to peacefully leave at the first opportunity.

Haswell went off to sulk and that night in his journal named the bay "Murderers' Harbour" (Voyages 39) in angry disgust. He wrote some nasty comments about Gray's organizational skills, and concluded by vowing never to go ashore again without being heavily armed. Interestingly, there is evidence that Marcus did not die that day but survived his wounds. It is possible that not all the Tillamook agreed with the decision to attack the boy, and took him into their care. Captain Francis Cross, a *Lady Washington* historian, discovered stories that have been passed down in the area of a Tillamook chief with especially dark skin which may very well be Marcus Lopius or one of his descendants. Let us hope the legend is true and the brave lad from Cape Verde went on to live many years among the natives of the beautiful Oregon coast.

The moment it was light the next day, on Sunday the seventeenth, Gray set out to leave the harbour without waiting for an ideal tide. His reasons were sound—there were hundreds of natives on shore that might attack at any moment and the *Lady* only had ten able men on board, since one was badly wounded and Marcus apparently slain. At first all was well as the sloop made her way to the narrow passage, but just at that moment the wind died and the tide turned against them. Captain Gray had to order the anchor lowered, and in shallow water the *Lady* was buffeted against the bottom of the harbour, sending waves as high as the upper rail of her stern, flooding below deck and giving such a violent up and down movement that her crew could barely manage to stand. It didn't take long for Gray to realize the seriousness of the predicament, and he ordered her to be kedged off. The longboat was taken out with a small anchor and rowed to the east. The *Lady* hoved to it, but the tide was draining too rapidly and their efforts proved useless. There was nothing to do but wait it out, as her rudder was slowly bent awry by the constant smashing against hard sand.

Another night passed, and heavy fog drifted in, enshrouding the *Lady* and making visibility difficult. Outlines of war canoes drifted in and out of the mist, and dreadful hollering and cries could be heard back and forth. The crew anxiously stood by the rail with muskets ready, when suddenly out of the gloom a heavily armed war party burst from the fog and bore down on *Lady Washington*. Still determined to keep friendly relations as long as possible, Captain Gray merely gestured that they had to keep away. We do not know the reason the native Tillamook did not heed his warning—it might be that they simply did not comprehend what he meant. Having only a few men in a grounded ship surrounded by fog, Gray decided a show of force was necessary and ordered three swivel guns shot at them. It definitely made his point clear, and the canoe swung well away from the sloop and vanished back into the mist.

The tide ebbed in favor of the sloop, she was lifted up into proper buoyancy once more and Gray was able to kedge off and sail as far away as possible from Tillamook Bay. Deciding to play it safe, he kept the *Lady* on a northward course into Washington for several days before daring more trading efforts, and sailed right past what was to become Gray's Harbour. He probably thought it was best not to try entering it at the time, due to the rather unpleasant experience of Tillamook bay.

On the twentieth of August, the *Lady* was near modern day
Moclips, Washington, mostly inhabited by the Quinault
and Chehalis tribes. A few canoes paddled up around ten
o'clock in the morning. Though the natives of the area had a
shaky start with traders—in 1775 there was an incident with
the Spanish that ended in several deaths on both sides—by
1788 things had calmed down and they were quite ready to
work with Gray. The area was full of wide sandy beaches
dissolving into a flat terrain of pleasant woods. Natives were
keen on copper, but grudgingly accepted the iron which
was offered instead and handed over several soft otter skins
for the *Lady's* hold at what Haswell describes as, "a very
reasonable rate" (Voyages 41).

The next morning, a group of local Quinault paddled up in
two whaling style canoes. They didn't have any sea otter
skins, but the crew of the *Lady* was fascinated by their
whaling tools and how serviceable they were. A few of the
men requested them, but the Quinault were not interested in
trading the tools—they were much too useful and valuable.
After a friendly parting, the *Lady* weighed anchor and
continued north along the thickly wooded coastline past
Kalaloch Rocks. In the distance glimmered a shimmering
green verdant island of curious shape—like a frolicking
fish. It was about half a mile by a quarter of a mile in size.
Haswell called it "Green Island" but there is evidence as

early as 1792 that the island was named "Destruction" and
it appeared under that name in all subsequent charts from
the nineteenth century to today. Most of Cook and Meares'
charts do not bother to even show the island, but using them
we know that the nearest reference points were what was
known as "Shoal Water Bay" during Haswell's time, and
Mt. Olympus which is now the Olympic National Forest.
Lady Washington sailed past the Olympic Mountains, as
her crew gathered in awe to gaze at the snow-capped peaks.
The weather turned foul for the next few days and the
sloop sailed by several promising harbours, including Cape
Flattery. There was a great deal of speculation amongst the
Lady's crew that one of the deep inlets might lead to the
sought after Northwest passage, and each man had his own
theory about which of the bays might be "the one".

The sloop dropped anchor offshore of what became Ucluelet
in British Columbia, Canada. It was a pristine area with
whales and all sorts of marine and animal life. The natives
of the area were the Nuu-chah-nulth. The only other traders
known to have been near Ucluelet before were Captain
James Cook in 1778, Captain James Barkley in 1787 and
Captain John Meares the month before in his ship *Felice
Adventurer*. The Nuu-chah-nulth were extremely clever, and
when a few of their canoes came up to the *Lady*, their chief
already knew several words in English and was confident
in his trading skills. The men on board the *Lady* were
delightfully surprised at the initial meeting, for the natives

arrived singing a pleasant melody, keeping stroke with the tune—a welcome change from the usual hostility or curious airs of the Northwest coastal peoples.

The chief politely waited to be asked on board the sloop, and clambered aboard without hesitation once the invitation was given. They had no sea otter skins in their canoes, but when Captain Gray explained what they were after, the chief immediately made opening trading demands that were overpriced in Gray's mind. Perhaps he was not used to extreme tactics in a barter system, or he wanted to see the furs before entering into any sort of agreement, so the natives went back ashore empty handed, but still cheerful about the meeting.

On Saturday, August 30, the wind became very calm and fog drifted in, surrounding the sloop. The current of the coast was very strong, and without realizing it, they drifted south right toward a wide ridge of rock which jutted up from the bottom of the sea and lay level with the water. One of the men on watch gave a shout, and the crew gazed with horror at a violent churning in the water where surf broke onto unseen rocks looming out of the fog. There was no wind to maneuver with, so Captain Gray called for the sweeps and all hands on deck to fend her off from being hulled by the sharp rocks. It was a tense moment as men manned the side, "there was scarce the hollow of one swell betwixt us and a watery grave," (Voyages 44). At the last moment, the mainsail

flapped, then spread under a gust of wind. Without wasting
a second, Gray used the momentary breeze to bring the *Lady*
clear of the rocks, learning first hand how dangerous it was
close in to the shore of an unknown coast that was poorly
charted. More natives in their canoes had circled round to
watch and flocked to the sloop once she was clear. Trying to
be helpful, they signed to Captain Gray that to the Northeast
was a harbour called Nootka sound, which was safer for
Lady Washington and had many furs to trade.

Taking their advice, and still worried that he was too close in
to shore, Gray launched the longboat to tow the sloop clear,
and several of the Nuu-chah-nulth in their canoes pitched
in as well. Together, they brought her to nearby Clayoquot
Sound before paddling back home, no doubt eager to tell the
story of how they had saved a foreign ship from grounding.

The natives of the area were quite used to fur traders, so
the next morning boatloads of fine sea otter pelts in canoes
were brought up to the *Lady* for inspection, lead by their
chief, Wickananish. He was originally from the Clayoquot
tribe that resided near Kennedy Lake, but was an expert
tactician who managed to ally himself with enough warriors
to conquer Tofino Inlet, the Esowista Peninsula, and Meares
Island. He was quick to recognize the potential profit of the
sea otter trade, and his people were fine boat craftsmen.
He arrived on board *Lady Washington* with his brothers,
"completely dressed in a genteel suit of clothes," (Voyages

45) and was a shrewd trader who passed over most of what the sloop had to offer. He had two interests—copper and firearms. Gray found himself a little embarrassed when facing the dignified chief and offering the pathetic trinkets which Barrell had supplied him with. The Clayoquot chief mentioned the names of several captains, and said that Captain Meares, who had stopped by only weeks before, had given him the fine suit of clothes.

The ever present problem of water persisted, so Coolidge took the longboat out and easily found an excellent landing in the area. The crew bemoaned their lack of trade articles, for there were plenty of sea otter furs, but the *Lady* did not have what the Clayoquot natives were interested in and Gray was loathe to give them firearms. It was a spectacular area to anchor in, however, and Haswell complained in his journal that they were not there long enough for him to have time to properly sketch its beauty. They hit another squall on their way out, and the fog held, making sightings impossible for days. It was a difficult coast to navigate at the best of times, with jutting peninsulas coming out without warning, and Gray often had to suddenly change course when the fog cleared revealing the *Lady* was too close to shore. They also had to be careful not to stray out to sea and run the risk of sailing right past Nootka Sound. There was a bit of trouble with thick kelp beds along the coast, and they had to disentangle the rudder a few times.

On Tuesday, the sixteenth of September, the *Lady* caught sight of Nootka Sound. Captain Cook had charted the area very thoroughly, and Gray must have been pleased to finally know exactly where he was. They had nothing to do but hope the natives of the area would be interested in some of the articles they had on board. It would be difficult to write back to Barrell informing the financiers that their money had gone for naught. In the evening, *Lady Washington* slipped into the sound, only to see a small boat coming up that was clearly European.

There was a tense moment as everyone hoped it was not the Spanish. Fortunately, an English voice bellowed toward the sloop and Captain Gray sighed with relief. It drew near and the men on board told Gray that there were two British brigs in a nearby cove, and offered to guide the *Lady* in, since passage could be a bit tricky with narrow waters and rocks everywhere. Grateful for a pilot, as well as relatively friendly faces, Captain Gray gladly accepted the offer, and breakfasted with the officers of the British expedition. *Lady Washington* anchored in Friendly Cove beside the 230 ton *Felice Adventurer* and *Iphigenia Nubiana*, who were the brigs mentioned by the men in the boat. They had caught up with Captain John Meares at last—he had been sailing up the coast a month ahead of them and was the one who gave Chief Wickananish his suit.

John Meares was around thirty-two years old when he met Captain Gray. The British explorer had been a lieutenant in the Royal Navy during the American Revolution, but changed to the merchant service after the war. He was familiar with the Northwest coast, having sailed it for two years before meeting *Lady Washington* in 1788. Despite the fact Spain had control of the area, Meares was determined to establish a British trading post on Vancouver Island. He was bold, clever, and had a dash of the romantic brigand in his demeanor.

Meares was no fool, and knew how delicate relations with Spain were at the time—not long after 1788 England and Spain were formally at war. His ships were flying Portuguese colours—made possible by Captain Meares' good reputation in the Portuguese held port Macao in China. The subterfuge would not only make the Spanish think twice before attacking, but also allow him the ability to evade the South Sea and East India companies.

Captain Meares was the sort that walked the edge when it came to rules, and often operated in a gray area between legitimate commerce and piracy. Despite runs of bad luck, he remained popular in Britain—there is always something fascinating about an adventurer doing whatever it takes to forward his own and his country's interests, even if a bit of red tape was broken along the way. His men did not always agree with his daring decisions, and there was an attempted mutiny shortly before they met Captain Gray's sloop. The ringleader ended up joining *Lady Washington's* companion ship *Columbia* for a brief time.

On shore were a few hastily constructed buildings forming a sort of defence. They weren't very impressive—nothing to Fort Ross which the Russians later built on the California Coast, but they did keep out the rain, and Haswell remarked they were, "tolerable" (Voyages 48). Captain Meares' main project was the construction of his own sloop—the first one built on the Northwest coast. It was about thirty-to-forty tons and not very imaginatively named *Northwest America*. The work had been started three months before, and by the time *Lady Washington* arrived, the sloop was nearly complete.

Captain Meares was, no doubt, quite pleased to have a foreign ship arrive just in time to witness the launch of his pet project, and wasted no time telling Captain Gray and the *Lady's* crew all about it. The captains and officers dined together, exchanging what news they thought was prudent. Captain Meares announced that he intended to winter in Hawaii—the previous season he had tried to stay on the coast, but the result was disastrous and twenty-three of his men perished from cold and hunger. It was not entirely a cordial meeting—after all Meares had fought against many of the crew of *Lady Washington* during the war. Even Haswell, whose families were loyalists, did not trust what Meares' said about the trade that season. The captain insisted they had been unable to procure more than about fifty skins, but the *Lady* had been informed elsewhere that the British holds were nearly full. Haswell describes, "on our smiling (for we had been differently informed) he said it was a fact upon his sacred word and honour, so intent was this gentleman in deceiving us that he hesitated not to forfeit his word and honour" (Voyages 49). Here we see again how new the *Lady* was at the fur trade—it was common practice not to tell the correct amount of cargo to other captains and even the expedition financiers. Both crews maintained an outer façade of politeness, however, and Gray decided to stay in Nootka Sound.

Scurvy was rearing its ugly head once more, and when Gray tried to negotiate with the natives for vegetables, they did not seem interested. Concerned, and no doubt wanting to do a bit of exploring on his own, Captain Gray took the longboat out to search for other villages, and ordered *Lady Washington* hauled ashore and her hull seen to. The sloop had suffered damage to her rudder leaving Tillamook Bay in such a hurry when Marcus was injured, and Nooka Sound seemed a safe enough place to repair her. It may seem quite drastic to bring the sloop onto dry ground, but in reality it was exactly what she was designed for and standard practice. With her small crew, there was no expert in ship repair on board, so on the nineteenth of September (or twentieth for the British who had come round the world from the opposite direction), Captain Meares sent over his blacksmith to assist with the rudder pintles and gudgeons that had been warped by continued bashing against the sand bar in Tillamook. They also carefully examined her hull, cleaned it, and caulked where needed.

As they were employed in their labours, a man snuck out from the shelter of the trees and beckoned to Coolidge. Intrigued, the first mate went over and discovered it was an Englishman. The man explained that he was John Green, the former boatswain of *Felice Adventurer,* and leader of the failed mutiny six months before. He had been locked up in one of the buildings constructed by Captain Meares, had managed to escape, and was hiding out in the woods. He pleaded with Coolidge to help him, "adding that he was well acquainted with the coast and the languages spoken on it," (Voyages 57). Coolidge told the second officer, Haswell, who was extremely skeptical of the mutineer, but they decided that Captain Gray ought to be informed. Meares had already foreseen his former boatswain's attempt, and had asked Captain Gray to give his word not to take any of the mutineers on board *Lady Washington.* Gray was a man of honour, but not without pity, and made sure that John Green had plenty of food and provisions, though he would not allow him on the *Lady.*

Captain Meares deemed his own sloop ready for launching, and the crews of all three ships stopped work to cheer on the maiden sail. *Lady Washington* gave little *Northwest America* a formal salute of guns, and the rest of the day, "was spent in festivity and mirth" (Voyages 50). The crew of the *Lady* had been seeing nothing but each other and a few Native Americans who didn't speak English for months—if you've ever been stuck with the same ten people for that long, you know how great it is to be able to go to a party with a new set! The next day repairs were completed and the *Lady* was hove off and anchored back out in the cove. Attention turned to gathering wood and water.

After the festivities surrounding *Northwest America's* launch, the attitudes of the two groups changed, and even suspicious Haswell enthusiastically recorded that, "an intimacy on a very friendly footing subsisted between the English gentlemen and ourselves," (Voyages 50).

As was usual in the day, Captain Meares, the first ship to leave, offered to take on board a packet of letters to China for Captain Gray. There was no postal service in those seas, so whichever vessel planned on going to a civilized port first would bring letters to deliver from captains who were staying in remote areas. The English did not end up delivering them, and for various reasons sent the letters back. This was extremely irritating to the crew of the *Lady*, but at least they were returned. Captain Meares left the cove, leaving *Iphigenia Nubiana* behind temporarily.

On Tuesday, September 23, the *Lady*'s crew were working hard to prepare for sea once more—filling water casks, cutting wood on shore, and rotating rigging. A few enthusiastic cheers came from those on land, and the officers on board *Lady Washington* saw their men frantically waving toward the harbour entrance and shouting. Coolidge and Haswell turned their glasses in that direction and sure enough another ship was limping in. She was in a sorry state, with her masts struck and topsails reefed, but she was still familiar. The *Columbia* had found them at last. Captain Gray, having returned from his scouting expedition, was informed and the longboat sent out to render assistance. By five o'clock in the evening, the damaged *Columbia* rocked gently beside the *Lady*, reunited for the first time since Cape Horn.

Her crew was desperately ill with scurvy and barely hanging on in an, "advanced state of that malignant distemper" (Voyages 51). A few of the men had died, and the masts had been struck to allow easier handling of the ship for those with strength left to man her. Captain Gray's original plan was to take the *Lady* out again as soon as she was fit for sea, but his duty was to assist the *Columbia* first, and Captain Kendrick was still in overall command of the two vessels.

Kendrick was less than pleased to find British anchored in the same cove—he was a staunch patriot and still despised England and everything to do with that country. It was probably for this reason that, when Gray told him about the mutineer hiding in the woods, Kendrick invited John Green to board *Columbia* once the English left the cove. After all—Gray had only promised not to have him on *Lady Washington*.

There were still repairs to be done on the *Lady*—mostly caulking work—which was not finished until the end of September. One year had passed since their departure from Boston, so *Lady Washington* fired a Federal salute of thirteen guns in honour of the occasion. The British replied with thirteen total from their shore battery and *Iphigenia Nubiana*. Their officers, along with the *Lady*'s, went on board *Columbia* to dine, and the crews took the day off for mirth and festivity. October was mostly rainy, and on Sunday morning of the twenty-sixth, Boston time, Captain Douglas' *Iphigenia Nubiana* was towed out of the cove and set off for Hawaii to winter in that tropical paradise. The American ships were alone in Friendly Cove, and John Green began service before the mast on *Columbia*.

Not particularly keen on following the British to Hawaii, and wanting to have a head start in the next season, Kendrick decided to give orders that *Lady Washington* was to stay all winter. No doubt inspired by the stories of Meares' successful construction of *Northwest America*, Kendrick eyed *Lady Washington* and considered rerigging her as a two masted brig right there in Nootka Sound, but was disappointed to find that they didn't have the proper resources available. Instead he turned his attention to building a shelter on shore, wanting to show up the English with an American building, which wasn't much of a success.

November came, and covered the cove in snow. Food was running low, so Haswell took a group of men hunting. They followed some deer tracks and hid behind rocks waiting for the animals to return. It wasn't much fun sitting in the freezing cold, but they managed to take down a few bucks. Many of the men were employed trying to create items that the Native Americans would actually be interested in. Neither ship had copper, but some natives expressed that iron chisels were of value, so the crew set to work creating enough to take out trading the next season.

It was a bit dull being in the same frosty cove for months, and Haswell wrote that the only interesting thing to do was go hunting, though the natives picked up the idea and began bringing over fish, deer, and oil to *Lady Washington* during the winter. They had a bit of trouble when some natives from a distant village made off with items from the *Columbia*, but the locals explained they had nothing to do with it and were at war with that tribe. Kendrick decided not to make a big deal about it—venturing far into a snowy wilderness when he wasn't even sure what village was responsible was not a good idea. They celebrated their first Christmas on the Northwest coast, and on January 20, 1789, Captain Gray decided it was best to make another inspection of the hull. The anchor was raised and hauling ashore had began when Kendrick on *Columbia* ordered a stop to it, asking what in the world Gray thought he was doing and insisting the *Lady* was fine where she was. Captain Gray dropped anchor again, and did what he could to refit her while still moored in the cove. The incident served to cause more friction between the two commanders.

By the end of January, word spread that a fur trade vessel was in Nootka for the winter, and native canoes began appearing offering skins. Most would only take copper or muskets, but a few were willing to trade for the chisels, so the *Lady*'s hold began to have a good cargo of furs. As February began, nearby villages which had been deserted during the harshest winter months began to fill, and Kendrick got a bit worried about the number of natives surrounding the cove—particularly for *Lady Washington*, who was small and appeared more vulnerable than his own vessel.

If there was one thing Kendrick liked, it was cannon—in his mind there could never be enough guns on board, so he immediately added a bulwark bristling with ports for the sloop and brought her extra cannon off the *Columbia*. We do not know an exact number of what was added to the sloop, but it has been estimated at four to ten three and six pounders along her sides and in the stern—Kendrick had grandiose plans for *Lady Washington* and no doubt wanted her to look more like the sloops of war he had seen during the Revolution than a relatively helpless trading vessel in hostile waters. The decision proved to be a wise one, considering the unstable nature of the areas to which she went, and it was not simply a matter of Kendrick enjoying playing about with guns—though that might have been an influence.

Not long after, *Lady Washington's* crew heard the ringing of *Columbia's* bell and shouting coming from the other ship, followed by billowing smoke—the worst nightmare of a wooden ship had come to pass, for *Columbia* had caught fire. The winter was bitter cold, and Kendrick was far from the galley, so he'd arranged for a brick heating stove in his cabin, and that was the cause of the fire. The *Lady's* crew manned the longboat and rushed over to help, just in time to stop the fire from reaching the magazine and blowing the *Columbia* into tiny bits. It took a while to quench the flames which were roaring up the rigging and sails, but the emergency was averted in time.

March came, and for some reason, John Green decided he did not want to ship aboard the American vessel *Columbia* after all. He would not sign the proper papers, so Kendrick put him back ashore. Every man on a ship had to pull his weight—it wasn't a pleasure cruise for passengers. On the eleventh, final preparations were made on the *Lady*, and her people were set to painting her crisp and bright for the oncoming season. *Lady Washington* received supplies she needed from the other ship, and sent over more iron from her hold in return as Captain Gray and Kendrick went over what was required for each vessel in case they parted again. Shining in her fresh coat of paint, *Lady Washington* gave a salute with her new guns, as the two vessels carefully left the cove back south to Clayoquot Sound. On the seventeenth, they were met in a canoe by Toteescosettle, a brother of chief Wickananish whom they had seen on their first visit. Trade went better with the chisels, and a few skins were purchased. Kendrick showed great respect for the chief, and even fired a cannon salute.

The next day, *Lady Washington* kedged deeper into Clayoquot Sound, and was rewarded by managing to purchase many skins. The officers ran off to do some shooting and brought back plump geese for supper. As the earliest merchant vessel on the coast that year, the natives were quite eager to trade with the sloop, even though the

Lady had no copper. Captain Gray met the local chief, Cleaskinah, who also went by the name Captain Hannah. The chief was an agreeable sort of man, who enjoyed having various ships come to his village, and impressed the second officer as being, "a very intelligent old fellow" (Voyages 67). They were able to trade for several furs from Cleaskinah, and parted on excellent terms.

Since he had plenty of furs on board of northern sea otters, Gray decided to postpone any more trading until sailing south along the coast, so he turned down several offers of pelts by the locals. As a result, there wasn't much to do save leisurely follow the *Columbia*, try for a bit of shooting at birds flying by, and in Haswell's case, sketch the coastline. As they continued, speculation started again regarding almost every inlet passed—could it be the mysterious Northwest Passage? Her crew gazed out, arguing about each dip of the coastline. Prudently, Gray ignored all suggestions to try out the various bays.

On the twenty-ninth, some natives came by to see the sloop, and were given a few presents. They were more timid than most along the coast, but returned in several canoes with salmon for sale and paddled along with the sloop for the rest of the day, chattering in their dialect. The natives had only been visited by longboats before, and were amazed at *Lady Washington*—she was the largest vessel they had ever seen and must have been pleasing with her colorful sides and massive mainsail. The sloop alternated between sailing, sweeps, and being kedged. One set of natives offered hand woven blankets for sale, which intrigued the crew of the sloop, as they hadn't seen anything like them before. The cloth was most likely created of white dog hair and cypress fibers. On the last day of March, the sloop had some trouble with rocks and a difficult wind—Gray had to make several tricky tacking maneuvers before the sloop was safe again.

Just as they were beginning to breathe easily, a sudden storm blew in and they could not get out to sea in time. All hands took in the sails before they could be ripped, and Gray brought the sloop back into the nearest cove to wait it out. The *Lady* anchored there for several days until the weather cleared; the squalls made Gray nervous, and he kept running in to shore upon threatening weather as they continued. One cove he tried seemed suitable, but Coolidge and Haswell recommended leaving, since a wind was bringing some heavy swells and they were in only five fathoms of water. Gray agreed with the officers and took the *Lady* back out to sea.

Every time the sloop tried to sail on along the coast, another dreadful storm would come and he was forced to make a run for a sheltered cove. It was dangerous to try sailing so close to the coast in that kind of weather, and the mainsail was almost constantly reefed so they made little progress. The next few weeks were almost as difficult as the *Lady*'s trip round Cape Horn—there was a constant stream of rain alternating with hail, and the wind blew in gale force as the sloop was violently tossed up and down. The crew could barely sleep, for Gray had to constantly monitor the weather and take in sail whenever it became necessary, then quickly carry all the sail she could handle as the weather briefly cleared. On one such an occasion, the sloop raced past Destruction Island on her way back, but that evening had to quickly take in both the jib and mainsail. The *Lady* was down to only her foresail for the rest of the night, until the forenoon watch when they reset the mainsail. Most of the work was done under lashing rain, heaving seas, and cold weather. The only consolation was that Gray knew the coast much better, having sailed in the area on his way north.

On April tenth, the skies cleared and Coolidge took the opportunity to go ashore and hunt some game. He gave Haswell quite a fright, because those on board *Lady Washington* heard loud shouting, then all the natives jumped into canoes and paddled as fast as they could out to sea. Fortunately, Cleaskinah was able to explain that they were only excited that Wickananish had begun a whale hunt, and the village was going to watch the fun. These were the days before television and internet; when something exciting happened, people dropped what they were doing to go watch—they couldn't just watch it later. Eager to watch the spectacle, and "curious to see them kill this large fish with such simple implements" (Voyages 77) Haswell jumped into the canoe of an obliging native, followed by John Treat, *Columbia*'s furrier, who also wanted to witness the hunt. They were paddled over to where the whale was lying quietly harpooned. Noticing that officers from the American sailing vessels were present, Toteescosettle offered a seat in his canoe to Haswell who excitedly clambered in. The canoe went straight up to the whale, and Toteescosettle, "gave him a deadly pierce and the enormous creature instantly expired," (Voyages 77) and was towed into the village.

All the Clayoquot were celebrating, and many offered to let Haswell and Treat stay, but although Haswell was interested enough to ask questions about the hunting, he wasn't keen on the native diet and decided to go back to *Lady Washington* for his supper instead. Their time in the area was a pleasant one, and Gray was able to purchase more otter fur pelts before setting off once more.

The *Lady* sailed by the familiar Uclulet area into Barkley Sound's Sechart Channel, which is in between Nettle Island and Howard Point of what is now known as the Broken Group. Tides proved a navigational hazard, and leaving the sound was more difficult than originally anticipated. Gray wanted to stay the night, but the two officers pleaded to go straightaway, rather than run the risk of a current dragging them onto unknown shoals and rocks. They sailed

as carefully as possible all night, and in the first light of
dawn saw the northern entrance to the harbour. Local
natives flocked round the sloop but had no skins, because
Wickananish had already purchased them to sell to passing
ships. Barkley Sound is rather like a horseshoe of water
with dangerous rocky islands in the middle of it. *Lady
Washington* had been among those islands, and at daylight
reached the northern wide entrance of the bay. She then
sailed south past the island dotted center to the other wide
entrance of the sound. If the wind was correct, it was an easy
harbour to go in and out of, but with the wrong wind a ship
could easily run aground in the treacherous cluster of shoals.

On Thursday the sixteenth of April, 1789, the sloop, escorted
by dozens of canoes, sailed on, but fell to leeward of the
harbour, and therefore had to, "man the sweeps to gain
an anchoring place" (Voyages 80). Fortunately a breeze
came up the next day which literally blew the *Lady* right
into the harbour. They found more natives, this time with
skins to trade, and added two more furs to their cargo. By
April nineteenth, the *Lady* went by the entrance to Victoria
Harbour, which Haswell was convinced lead to a Northwest
Passage, although Captain Gray wasn't interested in a young
officer's theories.

A chief paddled up to the sloop, and sold twenty good quality
furs for only five chisels apiece, and they waited overnight
because he said there were more that he could bring. The

current was so strong in the area that the sloop was pulled into the Juan de Fuca Strait. The natives had no problem finding them, and Captain Gray bought thirty pelts before running out of chisels to trade with. He decided to return to Nootka, and as they went north, chief Cassacan paddled along offering otter pelts. Gray had to sadly decline, due to the lack of anything to trade with, and it was maddening for the crew to see so many excellent furs available and having to be passed up just because they didn't have any copper or chisels on board.

The *Lady* sailed by Ucluelet on the twenty-second, and a storm was brewing, so Captain Gray carried all sail and raced north at what Haswell estimated to be nine knots. By afternoon, the sloop made her way safely to Friendly Cove in Nootka Sound, and was surprised to find Captain Douglas in *Iphigenia*—he had arrived from Hawaii only days before. He explained that Kendrick had anchored *Columbia* in a cove a few miles off. Captain Gray set out at once in the longboat to find the other ship, and soon after two officers of *Columbia* arrived to visit Captain Douglas and exchanged news with the officers of *Lady Washington*.

The small British sloop *Northwest America* arrived from Hawaii, but when Captain Gray returned from his visit to the *Columbia*, he brought news that the *Lady* should leave Friendly Cove and anchor with *Columbia* in Marvinas Bay, which became the favorite American cove in the area. The

larger ship had not even begun preparations to go back to
sea, and most of her cannon were ashore as a sort of battery
similar to the one in Friendly Cove. A building had been
constructed, and her crew had not been idle—there were
plenty of chisels ready for the *Lady* to take trading. Gray
immediately began gathering wood and water, as well as
making another inspection of the sloop's sea readiness.

On April thirtieth, 1789, Haswell went out shooting with
Captain Kendrick—apparently relations between them had
improved somewhat since their last angry exchange. The
captain had apologized and perhaps Haswell simply needed
time to cool off in order to accept it. They hiked up around
the sound for almost ten miles hunting and taking note
of the coastline. It was getting dark, so they put together
a quick shelter, and at dawn gathered up the game and
headed back to the ships. Haswell described the excursion
as amusing, and clearly both men were in good humour, for
when Kendrick decided to visit Captain Douglas, he asked
Haswell to accompany him, though Haswell wasn't even
an officer on his own ship any longer, and neither seemed
to think it odd. The *Northwest America* was gone, and the
main matter on Captain Douglas' mind was the fate of the
mutineer John Green, which Kendrick explained.

On May second, *Lady Washington*, now with more chisels
on board, sailed north as soon as she was resupplied. It was
an ill fated day, for the next afternoon a sail was sighted.

At first, Gray must have thought it was one of the British vessels, for they were the only other ships he had seen on the Northwest coast. Alas, looking through a glass proved the ship was flying Spanish colours. They had a choice—fight, run, or try to talk their way out. A booming shot echoed across the water, and Captain Gray decided on the latter course. The formidable Spanish vessel *Princesa* was allowed to glide up, and ordered the American captain to come aboard and explain himself. It was a nerve wracking experience for Gray as he stepped into the longboat and was rowed over to the Spanish ship. One wrong word and his ship and cargo would have been seized for the Spanish crown. In the brief time it took to reach the other ship, Gray must have been rehearsing what to say—it was like being pulled over for speeding by a policeman, only with far worse consequences.

Martinez, commander of the *Princesa*, opened with the obvious question of what an American sloop was doing along a Spanish coast. Captain Gray thought fast, smiled, and replied that they were close in to shore due to an unfortunate incident with the natives. He said that *Lady Washington* was part of an expedition commanded by John Kendrick, the other ship of which was in Nootka Sound, and had merely stopped for fresh water. Upon leaving their barrels briefly unattended, Gray told Martinez that the natives had made off with them. He needed to find material for new barrel staves so that they could continue on their way. This was at least a plausible story—the incident in Tillamook had proved natives tended to pick things up when nobody was attending to them, and a ship couldn't go anywhere without water containers. It was also partially true—Kendrick used the same excuse with the Spanish in his letter to them on May twelfth. Martinez was clever enough not to entirely believe the tale, but decided polite decorum would be the most prudent way of addressing Gray.

He wanted to make it plain that the Spanish patrolled the coast, and made a point of saying that there were two other large ships nearby. He had recently been in the north and was on his way back down the coast to keep an eye on things. The warning was conveyed in true Spanish style wrapped carefully in compliments and flowery language, but Gray took the point. When Martinez expressed that he was bound for Nootka Sound, the American knew the jig was up. The minute Kendrick's little fort, or the otter furs they had collected were discovered, the Spaniard's courteous behavior would have instantly disappeared.

The answer was right in front of him—either Captain Kendrick was going down, or Captain Douglas. If Gray could get the *Princesa* to make for Friendly Cove, instead of Kendrick's Cove, he knew that the Spanish would make such a to do about the British hold on the area that a couple of little American ships would be forgotten. For once, the insignificance of the newly freed colonies in European politics worked to the sloop's advantage. Martinez asked if there were any other vessels in Nootka Sound, and Gray seized the opportunity. He explained that there was a good prize waiting in that sound—the other ship anchored there was a British crew flying false Portuguese colours and had plenty of otter skins on board that they had collected trading along the Spanish coast. The effect was immediate—Martinez' eyes gleamed in anticipation, and instead of boarding the *Lady* and searching her, he gave Captain Gray some lovely presents of sugar, hams, and brandy before sending the Americans back to their sloop. The vessels politely exchanged gun salutes and parted ways—everyone on board gave a huge sigh of relief, and Gray probably broke right into that ham. Martinez did indeed end up paying a call on Nootka Sound, seized all Meares' vessels, for more had arrived while the *Lady* was gone, and even imprisoned some of their crews in what became an major international incident that nearly provoked a war.

Another gale blew up, and the *Lady* was driven along the coast as Gray looked in vain for a safe harbour until spotting Checleset Bay. He took the *Lady* into Nasparti Inlet by the Brooks Peninsula—a narrow two pronged bit of water that is shaped like a grasping hand. The area was densely wooded with tiny islands scattered here and there, and, for the most part, a sheltered anchorage for the sloop. When the weather cleared, *Lady Washington* pointed her prow out of the harbour only to see another ship—the coast was growing

quite crowded compared to her solitary wintering. It was the
brig *San Carlos*, only slightly larger than the *Lady* herself,
and consort to the *Princesa*. This time, when Gray heard the
cannon shot and saw Spanish colours hoisted, he decided
to leave well enough alone. The *Lady* showed a clean pair of
heels and sped off with a good wind behind her.

She continued at about five knots for the rest of the day—
sailing past the Scott Islands and east toward the mainland.
A fog drifted in to enshroud the sloop at just the wrong
moment—*Lady Washington* entered a treacherous part
of the coast, "craggy with low detached small islands and
dangerous sunken rocks...a very intricate channel" (Voyages
86). There were islands everywhere, such as Athlone, Price,
Goose, Swindle, Aristazabal, and the Harvey Islands. By
the time the fog lifted, they found themselves completely
surrounded by rocky protuberances with narrow channels in
between. Fortunately most of the water had plenty of depth
for the sloop, although there were large kelp beds which were
a problem for the rudder.

At around two o'clock, a canoe arrived with some natives
who seemed friendly. Haswell was intrigued by the fact
their language sounded completely different from Nootka
Sound. They were quite willing to accept the iron on board
Lady Washington, so over twenty furs were purchased.
The men in the canoe offered to show where to anchor, but
after following them, Gray decided it wasn't a good enough

harbour to risk the *Lady* in. The current proved stronger than anticipated and there was a brief moment of scurrying and quick sail manipulation before her course was set right. It grew too dark to continue, and the sloop had to sit, "closely hemmed in by the continent on one side and on all others with reefs islands and ledges" (Voyages 87). Needless to say, the watches were especially alert during that evening for drift. Every now and then the sloop would have to tack to maintain her position, and it was fortunate that there was no fog and the moon was bright. After a tense night, the *Lady* was met by natives in canoes of the Milbanke Sound vicinity—both men and women. The Americans were a bit horrified by the way they had cut their mouths to put in a piece of wood, but the natives themselves were cheerful and interested in the sloop. The *Lady* carefully made her way through what Haswell called a labyrinth of islands and shoals before heaving to for a much less stressful evening.

More canoes arrived the next morning as the *Lady* continued north, but when she halted, they also halted. Captain Gray waited for them to approach, but finally gave up and started on only to find they followed. As if part of an absurd game, he hove to and they matched it. Oddly, the natives then paddled to a rock, clambered onto it and stood waving fur pelts. Used to the canoes coming right up to the sloop, Gray was a taken aback, but ordered the longboat out led by Coolidge and an armed escort with presents. They rowed to the rock and tried to show that the *Lady* meant no harm and they only wanted to trade—giving a few things to the terrified native men on the rock to demonstrate good faith. After trying in vain to persuade them to approach the *Lady*, the boat crew went back to *Lady Washington* and explained that the natives were too shy to come near. Haswell guessed that it was because they were the first Europeans to come close to the shore there, and it is possible he was correct.

Probably still chuckling over the incident, Gray sailed for the Queen Charlotte Islands, which were just to the west of where the *Lady* was sailing, across a wide channel. The sloop only halted for two hours that night, so by the next morning on May sixteenth, she had covered quite a distance. Haswell described with rapture the beautiful snow-covered mountains and idyllic terrain of the area, "a vast number of sea otters continually playing on the water" (Voyages 89). They were in the vicinity of the Dundas Islands, and managed to shoot some wild birds to add to the *Lady*'s meagre supplies. Spirits were high on the sloop– they had found a fantastic harbour with plenty of game, though it was rather rainy. Haswell even managed to find a sort of cranberry to eat.

The natives they met decided it would be a much better idea to go collect some sea otters themselves than to inform the rest of the tribe. For the first time, the crew watched as the Native Americans took some otters who were, "yet warm with life" (Voyages 90), skinned them, dried, and generally prepared them to the sort of state furs were in when offered for trade. It was one thing to trade for perfect pelts, and another to watch as the playful creatures were slaughtered. That sort of occurrence was usual for the time period, and none of the crew would have been particularly moved, although we looking back find it distasteful.

Captain Gray skilfully sailed on through some tricky straits, "deep dangerous sounds with much broken detached islands and sunken rocks" (Voyages 91) as Haswell put it. They heard some shouting from the stern and ran over to find a canoe trying to follow as quickly as they could and shouting to come back. Gray stood in to shore and the canoe paddled swiftly over, extremely excited at seeing the sloop. The natives explained that their village had plenty of skins, but they didn't have any with them in their boat.

The chief offered to come on board to ensure they meant no harm, but the weather began blowing a gale and, as the second officer said, "it was madness to attempt to seek a harbour so late in the day and in such weather" (Voyages 91). There was a new moon, and that night was pitch black, so Gray shortened sail and hove to. The wind increased, but even in the poor weather a canoe managed to come out in the morning. It was an old man with a couple of lads who "maneuvered their boat with great skill" (Voyages 92). They were also quite plucky, for the waves would have made even surfers cringe. The solitary canoe decided it wasn't a good idea to get too close to the sloop—the water could have slammed them right into her hull. They pointed and shouted until Gray understood it was instructions to follow for a sheltered bit of sea. Sure enough, the sloop followed the boat round a point and into a quiet inlet.

The natives were Haida, and Captain Gray was able to purchase several skins and learned that the area was well populated. There were plenty of otters, and the natives were quite advanced and seemed friendly enough. The green fertile lands impressed some of the *Lady*'s crew, and Haswell began daydreaming about starting a colony on the island. His musings were cut short when Gray decided to take advantage of the wind and set out from the area.

On May twenty-third, near Bucareli Bay in Alaska, a few days later, the strong wind held and increased to the point where the jib and mainsail had to be reefed. During an attempted entrance to what appeared to be a cove, an unexpected gust of wind caused the *Lady* to be taken aback. Before Gray could rectify the situation, it was too late to bring her round properly in the narrow strait.

He tried to wear ship, and *Lady Washington*, creaking and groaning as Gray sweated, trying to get her round, swung her way in between the rocks—even one mistake meant the sloop would run aground. Her extra long bowsprit began scraping against the upjutting stone and in a horrible wrenching the jib and bowsprit were torn away by the rocks. A huge swell of surf lifted the sloop up and over, tossing her like a toy in between more cliffs. The wind was blowing so hard that the pine trees on shore strained this way and that. Haswell wrote that, "every surf that arose lifted us high in air and as it descended dashed us against the rocks with the utmost fury and to add to our distress the wind increased violently...every surge left us resting dry on the pinnacles of this merciless iron bound coast" (Voyages 93). They were hundreds of miles from Nootka Sound—the only place where help could be found, "every nerve must be strained to extricate us from this dire dilemma" (Voyages 94). The crew were absolutely terrified—it was every sailor's worst nightmare come true. Each man tried desperately to remain calm enough to do whatever he could to help save the sloop.

Haswell took a few hands, poised himself waiting for the best moment to jump across the lashing swells, and leapt to the nearest rock. He caught some hawsers and made them fast as every few seconds he and the other men were drenched as the *Lady* plunged down and sent a wave of freezing water over them. Coolidge was busy in the longboat making ready to kedge. Miraculously he managed to keep the small boat steady enough not to sink from all the water being dashed into it. He rowed out to the full length of the line before dropping the anchor. Little by little the *Lady* was hauled away from the rocks. As most of the crew were working on kedging her free, the rest desperately tried to clear the mess

of wood and canvas that had been the bowsprit. Gray hoped
to find a safer part of the cove to stop and examine the hull
for damage before putting back out to sea, but circumstances
intervened and he had no choice but to make a run for open
water.

The drenched crew—still shaking with terror and shock,
did the best they could while at sea to inspect the damage.
Fortunately, the hull appeared unscathed, though the rigging
was a complete mess. Once Gray was certain the ship was
safe, boats were lowered for further examination. Her yards
were struck and a quick jury rigged bowsprit was put into
place. There were bits of rock stuck into her sturdy hull, but
she was seaworthy.

Gray decided to limp back to Nootka Sound, hoping the
Columbia was still there and could assist them. Haswell
recorded in his journal entry how desperate their situation
would have been if the *Lady* had not been saved. Stories
had somehow got round that the natives were cannibals,
which wasn't true, but the crew believed it and weren't
keen to camp out on shore. The alternative of rowing back
was equally treacherous. Anyone who has read about the
Shackleton Expedition knows all too well the perils of trying
to go hundreds of miles in nothing but cramped small boats.
The *Lady*'s crew aptly nicknamed the inlet "Distress Cove."
On the twenty-eighth of May, the *Lady* sailed past the
Queen Charlotte Islands again, and were greeted by, "a vast

number of natives men women and children" (Voyages 95). They were a pleasant sort, and Haswell describes how they, "came off in great parade paddling off swiftly and singing a very agreeable air" (Voyages 96). It was a welcome change from the frightening incident in the cove. The local natives had an elderly chief called Cuneah, and the crew of the *Lady* was amused by the amount of power his wife and the other women seemed to have—they gave orders to the men and were as much involved in trade negotiations as their husbands. Captain Gray bought several hundred skins before sailing on. It was extremely foggy the next few days and they could barely see the land most of the time; observations became nearly impossible.

On June eleventh, Captain Gray found a large sort of inlet near the Houston Steward Channel in the Queen Charlotte Islands and sent the boat out to sound it—he'd learned his lesson about checking coves before entering. Coolidge reported back that it was around fourteen fathoms with a sandy bottom and would do well as a sheltered anchorage. It was custom in that area for the chief to do all the trade bartering for his tribe, so Captain Gray and Chief Coya negotiated for the purchase of more furs. Unlike some of the other areas of the islands, iron was not in such high demand. Instead they were more interested in European clothing. Coya was quite familiar with other fur trade vessels, and Gray named the inlet "Barrell Sound" in honour of the financier who had orchestrated the expedition.

Haswell went ashore to have a look around, and discovered a fortified rock retreat. It was called a tout, and the women and children would flee there when a battle was taking place. The only way up was a ladder which the refugees could pull up until it was safe. Coya's people came by the sloop selling fish and boiled gulls eggs. Like other parts of the coast, the natives took anything that was left lying around, but Gray decided it was better to turn a blind eye to it than risk trade negotiations, and the crew learned to be extra careful not to become negligent with their things. The *Lady* traded for all the skins available in the area, so it was time to move on. It was difficult to leave—as soon as they began making their way from the harbour, heavy swells swept them out of reach of the entrance. Gray finally had to temporarily drop anchor on the lee side of a large rock.

Haswell took the boat out and examined six miles of coastline, but found no suitable harbour. The coast was deep and rocky without much shelter, and the weather became stormy. Gray had no choice but to give it a try, so the *Lady* sailed past Cape St. James and Clarence Strait. The crew was disappointed not to have the opportunity to explore on shore, and made all sorts of wild surmises about each strait they passed, "large rivers and lakes may be found that may overlap the western bounds...that have their vent in our eastern coast" (Voyages 99). Haswell bemoaned the fact that fur trade vessels had to do charting on the go since commerce was the first order of the day, and wished an expedition could be formed whose sole purpose was a careful examination of the coast and search for a Northwest passage. The *Lady* made her way by foggy Scott Islands and Cape Cook. On June seventeenth a perfect wind sent the sloop right into Nootka Sound. Friendly Cove showed several masts—the *Princesa* of earlier with her consort *San Carlos* along with the London sloop *Princess Royal*. When the *Lady* was sighted by the Spanish fort and ships, a salute was fired in welcome, but Gray was worried that the Spaniard's arrival in Nootka Sound had not gone well, and Martinez might have turned his wrath on *Lady Washington*, so Gray continued on to where *Columbia* had been left in Kendrick's Cove. Martinez was well aware of Kendrick's presence and had even stayed aboard *Columbia* for a night, so there was no trouble after all.

Kendrick gave a welcoming gun salute as *Lady Washington* slipped into the cove. He had explained *Columbia*'s presence in Nootka by pleading storm damage to the Spanish, as well as adding in some truth—that his crew had been dying of scurvy when they arrived. He proceeded to do everything he could to ingratiate himself with the Spanish. His own son, who was an officer on board *Columbia*, entered Spanish service as a commander. John Kendrick, Jr. spoke fluent Español, and was willing to convert to Catholicism. Martinez was impressed and even more friendly to the Americans after that. It was not entirely an act of preservation— John Kendrick, Jr. was able to command his own ship much sooner than had he stayed in the American merchant fleet. He ended up quite wealthy with a lovely wife and extensive lands. There is no reason to believe he regretted the decision.

Kendrick and Gray immediately began repairing *Lady Washington*'s hull and replaced her bowsprit as best they could. Coolidge was cordially asked by the Spanish to accompany a brief exploration in the captured *Northwest America*, renamed *Santa Gertrudis la Magna*, as interpreter, and he accepted. Kendrick decided to leave Nootka Sound—the British ships captured from Meares had been sent with their crews for trial, and he wanted to be out from under the Spanish battery while they were still on friendly terms. The *Lady* did not go far—just south a bit to Clayoquot—but removed from scrutiny by the Spanish ships.

8: KENDRICK TAKES COMMAND

The decision to winter on the coast meant that both ships were woefully short on supplies, and Gray made it clear that the natives wanted copper for trading—an item both were without. One of the ships needed to go to China, sell what furs they had, and resupply properly with useful trade goods. Joseph Barrell and the financiers were growing increasingly anxious—it had been almost two years without a penny of return in their investment. The *Columbia* was larger and could hold more furs, while the *Lady* was ideal for close in sailing and trading. It became obvious that the sloop should remain while *Columbia* made a run for China. Captain Gray pointed out to Kendrick several times, and on no uncertain terms, that he wanted to sail for China as soon as possible. Kendrick, on the other hand, was eager to do some exploring. The problem was that the logical choice of ships did not correspond with the opinions of their commanders. The solution was obvious—it was time to swap vessels. Gray would take all the furs on board *Columbia* and head for China, while Kendrick took the smaller vessel for trading. It was a well reasoned decision, though naturally there was a bit of grumbling about it on both crews and an inevitable shuffling took place.

Haswell had gone on board the *Lady* to avoid Kendrick, and didn't fancy spending another few years with him, so he went over to *Columbia* with Captain Gray. Kendrick made a few other crew changes and brought along extra hands, which resulted in the *Lady's* crew becoming around twenty. We do not know exactly which men Kendrick brought along, but there are a few possibilities. The original 1787 manifest of *Columbia* included John Barber, William Bowles, Thomas Foster, Robert Green, and John Maud. We know that they transferred with Kendrick, because in 1791, they were listed as being crew of *Lady Washington* witnessing a land deed.

William Bowles was a Bostonian, born November nineteenth, 1766, so he was almost twenty-one when the expedition set out. His family did not have a tradition of seamanship, although they were passionate patriots. It is not clear why the young man decided to put to sea—perhaps it was for the adventure which awaited on unknown shores. He had a particular talent for sail-making, although it is unknown if he had the official sailmaker title while on board the *Lady*. After about five years on *Columbia* and *Lady Washington*, he shipped aboard other fur trade vessels, often returning home to Boston between seasons. There he met Mary Cruft, whom he married. Ironically it was while in command of her namesake's ship that he fell into trouble. In an attempt to succour a ship being attacked by some natives in Nootka Sound, the brave captain of *Mary* was hit by a poisoned arrow and slowly lingered to a painful death on May twenty-first, 1803.

Interestingly, Martinez had given Kendrick 187 sea otter pelts to sell in China, but instead of sending them with *Columbia* for Gray to dispose of, he kept them on the sloop. Perhaps he wanted an excuse to have furs on board should another Spanish ship stop the *Lady* on her voyage along the coast, "they belong to Governor Martinez" would have been an excellent story to explain her hold full of pelts. The *Columbia* had done next to no trading at all, so most of the over 1,000 furs on board had been collected by *Lady Washington*—quite an impressive number.

On July thirtieth, 1789, everyone was packing, transferring various types of cargo, and saying farewell. The next day, Captain Gray and Haswell saluted the sloop that had been their home for over a year and sailed toward Hawaii on their way to China and on around the world.

The family of John Kendrick, new commander of the *Lady*, had been seamen for generations, so it was natural for him to have joined the profession as well. He grew up in Harwich, Massachusetts, and had gone to sea by the age of twenty on a whaler. Kendrick didn't hold much store by book learning—his writing leaves much to be desired, and his math skills were negligible. He cared for every single member of his crew, even before the mast, but always wanted to make sure things were done just right. If he had to spend a month reordering a ship's hold personally in order to ensure all was in order, he would do it. He was an unusual

mixture of methodical and fiery. A staunch patriot during
the Revolutionary War, he had commanded a privateer
and spent time as a prisoner of war. When he was twenty-
seven, he married the lovely Huldah Pease, but never gave
up his love of the sea. Kendrick was a friend of one of the
clerks of Joseph Barrell, and even though he was getting on
in years, he was chosen to command the expedition. When
he left Boston in 1787, Kendrick was never to see his family
again, save for the sons that were also on *Columbia*. He
was a difficult man to fathom—even when he was still alive.
Some, like Gray and Haswell, were so irritated by his slow
decision making that they chafed at what they believed to be
poor command skills. Others admired Kendrick as a worthy
and great captain whose foresight was invaluable. As we
look back over his life, Kendrick did indeed have chillingly
accurate foresight, and he proved himself capable of being
an inspirational leader. He also made a great deal of errors,
easily lost his temper, and rubbed a lot of people the
wrong way.

Kendrick began heading north in the *Lady* past Cape Scott,
making for the Queen Charlotte Islands. He had all the trade
goods from both ships on board, and began obtaining furs
right away with little trouble. Like all their journeys, the crew
kept straining for possible glimpses of a Northwest passage;
it was almost an obsession of the time. Captain Kendrick
had never been along the coast before, and was fascinated
with all the inlets. After a few weeks, he changed course back

south—near where Captain Gray had met the Haida—and dropped anchor. Most likely someone on board told him about their good luck trading at the village, and he thought it worth visiting. Kendrick was very different from Gray in many ways, and one of them was his dress sense. We have records of all sorts of rather extravagant purchases of clothing on his part—he always wanted to look the part of commander. Taking advantage of sunny weather, he had some of the contents of his chest washed and aired. They were left out to dry, and promptly disappeared. If there was one thing you did not want to do, it was mess with Kendrick's clothes—normally he was very kind to the natives and even ordered Gray to treat them with respect, but taking his shirts? That crossed the line in his mind. Think of it like a woman with her designer shoe collection.

Kendrick roared at the natives still on the *Lady*, and at some men in canoes. In the wrong place at the wrong time, innocent chief Coyah came alongside to trade. He was met by a furious Kendrick, who demanded that the clothing be returned right away or there would be severe consequences. He seized the poor chief, along with his companion Shulkmase, and locked them in stocks made out of the gun carriages, sending the other natives ashore to distribute the message that if the stolen clothes were not returned immediately, *Lady Washington* would set sail with the chiefs still on board. The entire incident was one big misunderstanding; it was Haida custom to leave articles, like clothing, out to air if they were being offered as trade goods. The items would be taken home and tried, then returned. We do it all the time today—if you purchase a coat, then wear it for a few days and do not like it, you can return the item with your receipt to the store if the tags are still on. With the language barrier, Kendrick saw only a group of savages stealing his prize possessions. The natives saw the crew of the *Lady* as savages who had wrongfully detained and mortified their chiefs for no apparent reason. A few of the men who had taken clothing for examination brought the items back, but there were still a few things missing.

Kendrick demanded the natives bring all their furs to pay for the stolen goods, and thus secure the release of their chiefs. To the Haida, and in modern times, his actions were illegal and shocking. Kendrick basically took the chiefs hostage and demanded otter pelts as ransom. He was coming from an entirely different perspective, however. Imagine if you were particularly fond of an expensive coat, but it was splashed, so you left it out to dry on a line. If it was stolen, you might call the police and even go to court if necessary to retrieve it or its value. You would then want some recompense for the time and trouble the legal proceedings had cost. While that is a trifling example, it is the sort of position that Kendrick found himself in. In addition, Europeans did not consider the natives to be proper people, but almost slave level cannibals— Kendrick did not find it odd that he should lock them up on his ship or demand furs as tribute.

To add insult to injury, and have a bit of fun, Kendrick decided to teach Coyah a lesson. He whipped the chief, painted his face, and worst of all shaved his head—hair was a symbol of power and respect among the Haida. In short, there was no possible way that Kendrick could have humiliated the chief any more than he did. Today, such a proceeding would be considered barbaric and cruel, but to the Europeans of the eighteenth century it was highly diverting and normal. Kendrick sailed off figuring those natives would think twice before trying to steal anything else from passing ships. He was wrong—there was only one thing Coyah wanted—revenge. His position among the Haida was ruined, and he lived in shame for months. Due to sun exposure on the *Lady*'s deck he also became extremely ill. Kendrick's momentary loss of temper and quick laugh would cost *Lady Washington* dearly when they came near the Haida again. Coyah began plotting his retribution from the moment she sailed out of sight.

After the unfortunate incident, Kendrick took the sloop back to Friendly Cove to visit Governor Martinez, but that also might have been a mistake. The governor could not help wondering why Kendrick would give up the comfort of an ample cabin on the flagship for a little sloop. Why had the smaller vessel remained for a mission of discovery when the larger had sailed on? Once again, Kendrick managed to talk his way out of it, and asked permission to return to the coast after visiting China. Martinez maintained his politeness, and even requested a few items be brought from China, but his trust was shattered. The only reason Martinez did not seize the *Lady* right there was that he didn't consider it worth the trouble—things had gone ill since he'd seized the British ships, and the government wasn't entirely pleased with him. There were no official orders in Nootka Sound for him to take the sloop, and he needed allies at that moment. Martinez had been having his own problems with the native population—in a fit of anger he'd shot a well beloved chief, and was worried about the safety of the Spanish ships in the coming winter. The natives that had been helpful when *Lady Washington* was wintering in the sound—bringing regular food supplies to trade for, had stopped in protest to their chief's murder. There was no supply ship due to come for another year, so eventually Martinez had no choice but to evacuate before they all starved. Kendrick, sensing the Spaniard's changed disposition, took the *Lady* back out as soon as possible and headed for Hawaii.

The crew of *Lady Washington* had wanted to visit what was then known as the Sandwich Islands for a long time. It had been a difficult few years mostly in fog and cold—their only lengthy shore leave was in the snow covered Nootka Sound. When Kendrick announced they were sailing for the balmy islands, the crew gave a cheer—it took around thirty days to reach the islands, and they were welcomed into a warm tropical paradise. Pristine beaches with emerald waving plants stretched out along a shore full of friendly natives who brought gifts of fruit and flowers. Kendrick tried his best to keep it business-like. They were there to resupply on the way to China, not have an extended holiday. He had a look at the sandalwood in the area as a possible trade item as well. It was his first idea ahead of its time—he realized that the fur trade would not last forever. Eventually China would lose interest, or the coast would run out of otters. There had to be some other cargo that would sell in China, and the sweet-smelling sandalwood was a possible answer. He added some to the *Lady*'s cargo of furs, but alas the fur trade was still in its boom and would not wane for many more years. The sloop went to several of the islands and spent the winter there. The crew was extremely grateful that Kendrick had not chosen another freezing sojourn on the Northwest coast. In January of 1790, *Lady Washington* sailed for China and arrived on the twenty-sixth.

Lady Washington sailed up to Macao and immediately found that China was ringed with bureauocracy. The Portuguese held Macao, and were not willing to let the sloop proceed. Kendrick had assumed it was possible to sail in, sell a few furs, and thus have enough money to purchase what was needed for supplies. In desperation, he wrote to Captain Gray who was in Canton hoping for some advice and to find out what the going rate was for furs.

Macao at that time was a busy shipping area, with all sorts of European vessels as well as local Chinese. Here is a description from John Bartlett, who was on a ship that arrived right before *Lady Washington*, "we steered to the northward and eastward trying to find a passage through the islands as we could not get a pilot out of any of the China junks, of which there were two or three hundred in sight," (Adventures 290). After passing the islands, like Bartlett, the sloop anchored in the Roads. Captain Kendrick, though frustrated at the lack of opportunity to sell the furs, maintained a tolerable good humour.

A flurry of letters passed between Captain Gray in Canton and Captain Kendrick in Macao—Gray had found an agent, but it was difficult to sell furs in Canton. There were multiple official and unofficial duties to cover requiring ready money. Macao's regulations tended to be looser and easier to circumvent. Gray's agent refused to take on the *Lady*'s cargo, having trouble enough selling *Columbia*'s, but recommended John McIntyre in Macao. Kendrick sent an inventory of three hundred twenty whole pelts, sixty garments, and one hundred fifty fur pieces to McIntyre. The weather turned foul, so the commander took the sloop on a quick run to Lark's Bay, which was known as Dirty Butter Bay in 1790. It was slow going selling even two-thirds of the cargo, for which he received 18,000 dollars.

Luck turned against him—Kendrick fell terribly ill and nearly died. As he was tossing with fever, Captain Gray completed the *Columbia*'s cargo of tea, silk, and other items. Although he had orders to stop in Macao and pick up letters for Barrell and the financiers, Gray did not bother. He was fed up dealing with Kendrick and merely went right on by Macao on his way back to Boston, ignoring the commander.

The news was brought to Kendrick as he lay ill in his cabin and it did not improve his mood. Gray was able to tell the financiers a completely biased story and turn Kendrick's name to mud. There were a few legitimate complaints against Kendrick, but most of his decisions had been logical and for the best. As a result of Gray's report, untempered by any letters from Kendrick, the financiers wrote the *Lady* and her captain off as a lost cause. Alone in Macao with his command basically stolen out from under him, Kendrick had some decisions to make. He could try to fill the *Lady* up with a cargo of Chinese goods and sail for Boston, but the reception was bound to be poor, and the financiers might refuse to pay him any percentage after hearing Gray's tale of woe. He would lose almost all chance of another ship and would be looking at languishing in Boston without a command. Another option was to sail for the Northwest coast as quickly as possible, hoping to meet up with *Columbia* if she were to return, and try to re-form the expedition. It was unlikely that Gray would co-operate, and for all Kendrick knew, Joseph Barrell might give Gray orders to take over the *Lady* if they should meet. The third and final possibility was to upgrade *Lady Washington* as much as possible and take her out independently, working off the debt to Barrell on his own.

Given the alternatives, that is precisely what Kendrick proposed, "I will take the Brig on my own account from the sixteenth of April, 1790, and abide by all losses and gains from that date; for which I will allow you the sum of fourteen thousand dollars with an interest of twelve percent from that date until payment is made," (Nokes 124). The letter gave him three years to pay Barrell—which was the equivalent of another trading season. Kendrick could work off the debt, guaranteed of a ship, before returning home and clearing his name. To that end, he needed something more serviceable than a mere sloop.

For years, the commander had wanted to convert the *Lady*'s rig, but during the winter in Nootka there had not been the resources to complete such a transition. Kendrick put nearly the entire profit of the first season into refitting *Lady Washington*. He chose to try his best to convert the sloop to a brig and leave for the coast. If he could procure full cargo and make it back to China early in the season, he would beat the other fur trade vessels, and there would be no need to languish in Macao pleading for a buyer.

He still had a crew to pay, supplies to purchase, and proper trade goods to bring on board, so he ended up having to borrow funds off Captain Douglas. The British captain who had sailed with Meares' did not do it entirely out of the goodness of his heart—after the disaster of trying to sail under a Portuguese flag, he had purchased the American ship *Grace* and retained her registry, deciding that an American flag would be safer. Kendrick gave permission for Douglas to temporarily sail with the *Lady* to reinforce the farce. Even so there still wasn't enough funding for *Lady Washington* to return to the coast—Kendrick was forced to use some of the money from selling Martinez' furs rerigging her.

It was a dangerous move, but his credit had run out, and the ship couldn't sail without being completed, so it is understandable. The immediate need no doubt overshadowed the problem of explaining it to the Spaniard later. Most ships with fur pelts had arrived months earlier than the *Lady*, so the ports were saturated with furs that would take some time to sort out. No matter how fine a cargo she had, the problem was that Kendrick had simply arrived too late in the season to make a profit.

Shore leave in Macao could be dangerous, for there were plenty of cut-throats in the harbour and murders were a common occurrence. Kendrick had to keep strict watch for plunderers who would sneak on board anchored ships during the night and make off with cargo. While it was much closer to civilization than the Northwest coast, Macao was still definitely not Massachusetts.

Since it was rather cramped on board *Lady Washington*, Kendrick took a house on shore, but it did not go well. He was known to be in debt, and the local Portuguese authorities liked to continually inform him of it. On one occasion, his house was broken into and rummaged through. After being openly arrested and mistreated in the street by some guards, he decided it wasn't worth it and moved back aboard the sloop.

It took some time for the *Lady* to be converted into a two-masted vessel. The majority of historians believe she was turned into a brigantine, which is a square-rigged vessel with a fore and aft mainsail. Maritime terms in the eighteenth century were a bit sloppy compared with current more precise language. Snow, brig, and brigantine were considered interchangeable, and from then on other captains seeing the

Lady would call her by a random assortment of those terms. Kendrick continued having funding problems, and her representative McIntyre found selling her entire cargo nearly impossible. Rather than sit around for another few months in Macao, Kendrick decided on a risky yet possibly rewarding course of action. If the Chinese were so fond of sea otter furs, what about other nations nearby? Japan wasn't too out of the way, and Kendrick didn't mind that it was technically a closed country at that point; the idea of being first to make the attempt fascinated the captain.

In March of 1791 *Lady Washington* and Captain Douglas in the sloop *Grace* set out for Hawaii; they sailed in company briefly until a squall blew up. Kendrick decided to use it to his advantage, and set off for Japan. He arrived at the Kii peninsula on Honshu asking for shelter from the dangerous storm. Being a hospitable people, the Japanese granted permission, though were concerned and word was passed that an American brigantine was in the area. The *Lady* anchored near Nagasaki—closed country or not, there was no way to suppress the fascination that her arrival caused. She was surrounded by fishermen and almost anyone who owned some sort of water craft. A few Japanese even came on board to look around and try some of the strange Western food. They called Kendrick the "red-haired barbarian" and his arrival was quite the event. Though he tried to sell them in his otter pelts, they had no interest in the soft furs. With nothing else to be done, Kendrick decided to gather wood and water before sailing for Hawaii, disappointed that the Japanese did not want the *Lady*'s cargo. At first the crew's shore parties did not cause any problems—in fact people stopped to watch with amusement how the officers hunted local fowl with such odd looking dogs. Kendrick forgot one important thing—Japan was not the Northwest coast. He was in a highly advanced civilization—not the wooded peninsulas of a wilderness. The trees of Japan were highly cultivated works of art, and when men from the *Lady* began gathering wood, there was a nasty incident. Chopping garden trees down in Japan was similar to digging up a neighbour's prize rose bush for a bonfire. The owner of the tree in question was absolutely furious, and came at the crew of the *Lady* quite violently, as any of us would have done to trespassers hacking up our garden. Unable to comprehend what he was saying, the crew fired a gun in the air to warn the man to back off. The owner went straight to the authorities to complain, and a group of Samurai were dispatched to deal with the situation. When Kendrick heard what happened he decided it would probably be best to leave before anything worse came to pass. He sailed away from Japan, watching the jewel-like islands sink into the distance.

The brigantine was still in debt and carrying a cargo of furs that he could not sell. At this point historians differ—some assert that *Lady Washington* sailed straight for the Northwest coast, and *Grace* for Hawaii.

Others believe that they did sail in company to Hawaii, but *Lady Washington* left after a brief resupply stop. Kendrick was not entirely sure what to expect from his new officers and crew. The time wasted in Japan caused him to be late arriving on the Northwest coast—he did not make it until thirteenth of June, 1791, and his run of bad luck continued.

Kendrick needed many furs as quickly as possible, so his thoughts turned at once to the Queen Charlotte Islands where both he and Captain Gray in *Lady Washington* had found plenty for reasonable rates. Trading went well at first, but word spread to the exiled chief Coyah that Captain Kendrick had returned; he was the chief that had been humiliated and lost his position due to Kendrick's explosion of temper over some clothes going missing. Still not realizing the seriousness of his mistake, Kendrick took the brigantine to what he called Barrell's Sound—most likely the Houston Steward Channel—the exact place he had injured the Haida chief two years before in 1789. Coyah gathered his supporters, and re-inflamed the passion over Kendrick's cruel joke.

If Kendrick had heard of the incident in 1785 with the ship *Sea Otter*, he might have thought more carefully before bringing the *Lady* back. The captain of *Sea Otter*, a Scotsman named James Hanna, arrived in Nootka and decided to play a joke on a local chief. He put gunpowder under a chair, then invited Chief Maquinna to sit down on it. The poor man was catapulted into the air by the blast, and in retaliation the Nuu-chah-nulth furiously boarded *Sea Otter* and a desperate battle was fought, resulting in a high death toll. Without knowing it, Kendrick was facing a similar situation.

The morning of the sixteenth of June, some natives in canoes came up with furs as usual and Kendrick welcomed them. More and more canoes began to arrive, and Kendrick did not think anything of it—the area was densely populated and it was usual to have the water covered with native craft. A few members of the crew were convinced that Kendrick had been drinking and wasn't entirely himself. He was a bit short of temper that day and lashed out. Whether he was just having a bad day, or was drunk we do not know.

He had ordered the arms chest overhauled, and the gunner had just finished working on it, so the keys were still in the chest. Glancing around, the gunner was not keen on the numbers of natives that were coming on board and complained to the captain, who was standing nearby.

Kendrick began roaring insults, and some narratives claim he even struck the gunner. It was a similar situation to when Kendrick and young Haswell had fought, for the captain shouted that the gunner had better get off the quarterdeck and shoved the man down the ladder. Taking advantage of this angry exchange, Coyah's men spotted the open and unguarded arms chest. Coyah pulled out the keys, whirled on Kendrick and grinned, dangling them in his face. The chief pointed at his legs, then the gun carriages, indicating the reason for the revenge was his imprisonment of earlier. As if by prearranged sign, a dreadful whooping was taken up and Haida swarmed on board, brandishing knives. Before the crew of *Lady Washington* could react, they found blades at their throats. The natives sent her crew down below, removing bits of clothing they found interesting, like cocked hats. More natives thronged aboard, "the women... more courageous than the men," (Adventures 321) led by a fierce Amazon-like warrior, presumably Coyah's wife, who shouted encouragement to the fray.

Kendrick watched in horror as the brigantine was taken over by Haida. He did not blanch, but wrenched out a marlinspike and brandished it, looking toward Coyah. He tried reasoning with the chief, but to no avail—the Haida wanted his revenge. Knowing there were pistols in his cabin, Kendrick began edging his way toward the hatch. Coyah decided to oversee the distribution of copper and jumped down onto the main deck. Siezing his opportunity, the captain tackled him. They tumbled to the bottom of the companion way, and the native slashed at Kendrick with his knife, ripping his opponent's shirt, but the captain dodged just in time as the blade tore its way over his skin. They grappled each other and Kendrick managed to free himself and made a mad dash to his cabin. He dove inside and seized a musket and brace of pistols.

The officers had not been idle and had rummaged around below to find a couple of firearms. They reorganized and upon hearing Kendrick's shout of, "follow me!" (Adventures 321) charged on deck, firing as they went. Taken by surprise at such a sudden and fierce resistance, Coyah decided that retreat would be prudent, "the fighting was furious and gory, but of short duration," (Cross 164). After a few minutes of battle, the Haida began paddling back to shore. Only the proud, fearless woman remained shouting insults before jumping into the water. Some of the *Lady*'s crew made it to the arms chest and one of them shot her before she made it safely ashore.

The main deck was a sorry mess, and the furious men of *Lady Washington* pulled out all the muskets from the arms chest. Like the aftermath of Pearl Harbour in World War II, when friendly planes were being shot at purely as a result of frayed nerves, the *Lady*'s crew fired at anything that moved on the water. Her cannon were rolled out and put into action, and though figures vary, we can estimate that around twenty to thirty Haida were slain.

Miraculously, though there were a few cuts and bruises, none of her crew were killed. Kendrick up anchored and headed for friendlier Clayoquot Sound. A ballad about the incident has been handed down, originating during the fur trade era, which has become quite well known. It tells a colorful version of events, and there are many variations.

The original author has yet to be determined, although due to internal references to "our ship" it is assumed to be a member of the *Lady*'s crew. We know that, within a year, word had spread throughout Macao and the Northwest coast about what had happened— whether that was due to this ballad or simply hearsay is unclear.

Come all ye bold Northwestmen who plough the raging main,
Come listen to my story, while I relate the same;
'Twas of the Lady Washington decoyed as she lay,
At Queen Charlotte's Island, in North America.

On the sixteenth day of June, boys, in the year Ninety-One,
The natives in great numbers on board our ship did come,
Then for to buy their fur of them our captain did begin,
But mark what they attempted before long time had been.

Abaft upon our quarter deck two arm chests did stand,
And in them there was left the keys by the gunner's careless hand;
When quickly they procuring of them did make a prize,
Thinking we had no other arms for to defend our lives.

Our captain then perceiving the ship was in their power,
He spoke unto his people, likewise his officers;
Go down into the cabin and there some arms prepare,
See that they are well loaded, be sure and don't miss fire.
Then down into the cabin straightway we did repair,
And to our sad misfortune few guns could we find there;
We only found six pistols, a gun, and two small swords,
And in short time we did agree "blow her up" was the word.

Then with what few firearms we had we rush'd on deck amain,
And by our being resolute, our quarter deck we gain'd;
Soon as we gain'd our arm chest such slaughter then made we,
That in less than ten minutes our ship of them was free.

Then we threw overboard the dead that on our deck there lay,
And found we had nobody hurt, to work we went straightway;
The number kill'd upon our deck that day was sixty good,
And full as many wounded as soon we understood.

'Twas early the next morning at the hour of break of day,
We sail'd along abreast the town which we came to straightway;
We call'd on hands to quarters and at the town did play,
We made them to return what things they'd stolen that day...

And now unto old China we're fastly rolling on,
Where we shall drink good punch for which we've suffered long;
And when the sixteenth day of June around does yearly come,
We'll drink in commemoration what on that day was done.

And now for to conclude, and make an end unto my song,
Success to the commander of Lady Washington!
Success unto his voyages wherever he may go,
And may death and destruction always attend his foe.

Kendrick passed Nootka Sound, and dropped anchor in Chastactoos, which he renamed "Safe Retreat Harbor." Though there was a definite Spanish influence over the area, the captain's vision was for Americans to one day colonize the coastline. To that end, he contacted Maquinna, the local chief, and on July twentieth, 1791, he purchased, "all the land, rivers, creeks, harbors, islands, etc," (253 Bancroft) in the area for ten muskets. He ceremoniously had the deed written up, and six influential native leaders made their mark, along with ten witnesses from the *Lady*.

Howel certified the document, and the brig sailed on.
Kendrick stopped and purchased more land deeds on August
fifth and sixth, each for a few rifles and some powder, with
occasional other items tossed in as well, such as sail cloth.

He was not taking complete advantage of them—for he
was careful the contract included permission for the
Nuu-chah-nulth to continue hunting and fishing in the
areas with no interference.

He arrived in Clayoquot Sound by August eleventh,
purchasing otter skins for, "muskets, iron, copper and
clothing" (Voyages 242). The Spanish were far from
pleased—he was supposed to have checked in at Nootka
Sound to announce his intentions. Kendrick knew he owed
8,000 dollars to Martinez, so he tried his best to avoid them.
Since he had spent so much time at Clayoquot, he decided on
a specially important land purchase—eighteen miles square
from the native village Opisitar. The trade was made with
full ceremony. The chiefs, as well as the captain of *Jefferson*,
another American ship anchored nearby, were present.
One of the men on *Jefferson*, James Tremere, also witnessed
the deed. There are contradictory reports as to whether
Columbia was present.

On August twenty-ninth, wanting to know how he stood
with the financiers, Kendrick took a boat out and by evening
came on board his old ship *Columbia*. Some of the crew were

happy to see him, such as young Hoskins. They certainly had plenty of stories to exchange—Kendrick told of his adventures in Japan as the first American flagged vessel in the islands. The next morning, Captain Gray and Hoskins returned the visit and breakfasted in a small building that Kendrick had fortified and named "Fort Washington" which he'd had a month to construct. The two ships were faced with their first rivalry, for the natives of the area had sold almost all their skins and announced that they would trade the rest to whichever commander gave the best price.

September was pleasant weather, and boats often went back and forth between the two Boston vessels. On the sixth, *Columbia* up anchored and bid farewell. Kendrick sighed with relief—he had been a bit nervous that Gray had orders to seize *Lady Washington* on sight. While the financiers were displeased with what seemed to be happening, they still considered him captain of the *Lady* and hoped for some financial return. Gray came back after only a couple of weeks because of bad weather, so Kendrick decided to leave for China. To avoid running into the Spanish, Kendrick took the advice of the natives and used backwater routes in the dead of night to take the *Lady* out of the Sound and set a course unhindered for Hawaii. After such poor results from the furs, Kendrick wanted alternate trade goods to offer the Chinese. He set several of his men on shore of the tropical paradise, with orders to search out pearls and wood and have them ready for when he returned.

Lady Washington dropped anchor near Macao on December seventh, 1791, with a thousand otter pelts, only to find there was a prohibition against selling them. There had been an incident between the Chinese and Europeans, prompting an embargo. Without any ready cash for supplies or the needs of the brigantine, Kendrick had to sit for three months doing nothing until the ban was lifted. Finally, in March, 1792, he was able to sell the cargo for 21,000 dollars. Kendrick wanted to go to Canton, because he had heard it was cheaper to refit a vessel there, but the Chinese were still leery and refused permission.

After some trouble, Kendrick managed to talk with a man on board a brig bound for the East coast, and got a letter through to Joseph Barrell. It explained the situation—how there had been difficulty selling the first cargo and that the ship was now badly in debt. He commented that Gray had disobeyed orders and sailed for Boston without stopping to receive dispatches, and apologized for not being able to send funds or a report back.

He asked for clarification—was he solely the captain of *Lady Washington*, under his own terms, or was the *Columbia* still under his command as well. He strongly requested that Barrell sell the *Lady* and her concerns to him for 14,000 dollars, which was a reasonable price considering she was eventually sold for only 1,300 dollars. Kendrick went on to remind Barrell that the alternative was to consider him still in command of the expedition, in which case he required his back pay and a commission of the *Columbia*'s cargo. This was not selfishness; he wanted to know how the situation stood and needed some cash to get the *Lady* out of debt in order to purchase supplies. He also addressed some nasty rumors Captain Gray had been spreading around, "you have been told many untruths respecting the voyage, and matters have been represented in a wrong light," (Voyages 472).

He allowed Captain Donnison, commander of the merchant ship *Washington* of Providence to borrow the *Lady*'s new boat *Avenger* to go ashore in. There has been some confusion caused by a tender built for the *Columbia* which was named *Adventure*. The tiny sailing tender of *Lady Washington* in Macao was either *Venger* or *Avenger* according to logs.

An interesting aspect of being in a commercial center was the amount of turnover in the people on board. *Lady Washington*'s officers remained the same, but many seamen went from one ship to another in the harbour depending on whether or not they wanted to leave. John Hoskins came aboard the *Lady* during December and January of 1791, but got tired of sitting idly in the bay, so he promptly moved onto the snow *Eleanore* which was up anchoring for the Isle of France.

In September, 1792, Kendrick set out, intending to winter on the Northwest coast and have a head start on the season. After sailing four days, the brigantine found herself right in the middle of a typhoon—worse than any weathered round Cape Horn. *Lady Washington* was tossed to and fro before a specially massive wave capsized her. Water seeped in and the brigantine began sinking under the weight of her own rigging. Drenched in the pouring rain, Kendrick gave the order to cut any excess on the masts to right her. The crew hacked at the lines, as her sodden canvas came loose and was flung aside in the raging seas. The next few hours were spent trying to keep her afloat and pump her dry. The tiny *Avenger* had not been so lucky.

At last the storm subsided and the *Lady* limped back to Macao. Along the way, Kendrick spotted less fortunate vessels who had sunk, and picked up over thirty Chinese survivors. The brigantine barely managed to arrive in Macao and had to begin refitting all over again—the last thing she needed while already deeply in debt. Some of her officers had to pool their funds in order to make her seaworthy. After a month's delay, she set out for Hawaii.

Kendrick, though growing increasingly discouraged, decided to send copies of the Northwest coast land deeds to Joseph Barrell and Thomas Jefferson to encourage an American settlement there. Barrell was mildly impressed, but too busy to do much about it, although he did publish a few pleas for settlers. Jefferson was also intrigued, and stored up the idea which culminated in the 1805 Lewis and Clark expedition.

Up until then, Kendrick had acted as supercargo on *Lady Washington*, but it was clear that finances weren't his area of expertise. As a result, John Howel became supercargo instead. He liked to try new things—Howel had been an Episcopalian minister, journalist, and clerk who travelled all over the world. He was keen on another voyage, and the perfect choice. He wasn't much of a seaman, but was a shrewd businessman who enjoyed being on board ships.

James Rowan also shipped on *Lady Washington* as first mate—he was an experienced sailor and wanted to have an opportunity of sailing along the Northwest coast.

This time the weather was quite pleasant on the voyage to Hawaii. Upon arriving, Kendrick sent for the men he had left on Kauai, but unfortunately they had either shipped aboard other vessels or deserted entirely and he returned to find no waiting cargo additions. Undeterred, in true Kendrick fashion, he set out to do it himself and properly. He gave permission for the crew to go ashore, which they instantly availed themselves of, and he set off to trade for items that might be useful in China. He managed to exchange some guns for pearls, but it took a bit of time. Kendrick wanted to make sure that he had a cargo worth enough in China to get the brigantine and himself out of debt.

He tried searching for alternate goods—ambergris, which is an element of perfume, pearls, and even a feather cloak. He gave out more muskets, as well as the *Lady*'s stern chasers. Kendrick loved guns, and had added the additional ones himself, so it shows how determined he was to lower the *Lady*'s debt that he was willing to part with them. Howel found quarters on the brigantine cramped and instead went to live on shore with King Kamehameha until *Lady Washington* up anchored. The two got along well, and the supercargo ended up with the nickname "Padre Howel" since the brigantine stayed for quite a while in the islands.

The *Lady* returned to the Northwest coast in 1793-4 to trade for more sea otter furs, and Kendrick was able to see his son who had joined the Spanish fleet. Due to lack of journals and logs, it is uncertain how long the brigantine was on the coast that season. It was a successful venture, for Kendrick arrived in Hawaii on December third, 1774 with a good cargo of furs.

12: The Death of Kendrick

It was common practice for European vessels to act as mercenaries in the tribal wars of the Hawaiians, and two British vessels had been part of such a war— on December thirteenth, *Jackal* and *Prince Lee Boo* sailed into Honolulu where the *Lady* was anchored. Kendrick and his officers were dining together in the stern cabin when the newcomers were sighted. As usual when entering a port in celebration, there was an exchange of salutes. It was as normal to them as a distant train whistle or car driving by is to us. The officers were not at all perturbed by the sound of cannon, until the *Jackal*'s guns boomed, and Captain Kendrick glanced in horror to see the *Lady*'s stern glass and wood smashed through before being slammed by the concussion of a blast of grapeshot. Debris and broken bits of glass fell like nightmarish snow onto the bloody scene.

Smoke cleared to find the gallant captain dead and his companions severely injured. Captain Brown and Alexander Stewart of *Jackal* quickly claimed it was an accident— they had not realized one of the guns was still loaded after the action the ship had been involved in. There is plenty of room for speculation on the matter, for clearing guns after a battle was routine, and it seems unlikely that it would have been overlooked—it is possible that the "accident" was deliberate murder. Kendrick had made quite a few enemies, and many of the British blamed him for the humiliation and capture of Captain Meares' ships. We shall never know, and if there is one thing to be learned from history, it is that simple human error is not to be underestimated.

Work commenced immediately to repair the *Lady*, and medical treatment found for the wounded men. John Howel arranged a proper burial for the captain. His body was taken to a grove of coconut palms near Honolulu harbour with the permission of Howel's friend King Kamehameha. The funeral was a curious affair—ceremonially garbed Hawaiians stood side by side with the crew of *Lady Washington* and men from other vessels in the harbour as Howel read a funerary service over Kendrick from the 1662 Book of Common Prayer. Here is an excerpt: "in the midst of life we are in death: of whom may we seek for succour, but of thee, O Lord, who for our sins art justly displeased? Yet, O Lord God most holy, O Lord most mighty, O holy and most merciful Saviour, deliver us not into the bitter pains of eternal death," (Books).

Though many have searched for the location of Kendrick's grave, including the Hawaiian Historical Society, State Historical Preservation Office, National Memorial Cemetery of the Pacific, and even the office of the Commander in Chief of the United States Pacific Fleet, it has not been discovered. Somewhere among the honoured fallen of the 1941 attack on Pearl Harbour lies Captain Kendrick of *Lady Washington*— the first American to be shot and buried on that island. The event has sometimes been referred to as the first December seventh, indeed the irony of the matching months is quite intriguing. Kendrick had not managed to return to China to pay Barrell or the *Lady*'s debts, and never returned home to Huldah his wife who waited patiently in New England.

With Kendrick's charismatic command lost, the crew had a brief time of reorganization. Howel took over the financial concerns and decided the best thing to do would be run for China and get the brigantine out of debt as quickly as possible. The first officer, James Rowan, took command of *Lady Washington* and skillfully sailed her to Canton. Previously, the brigantine had always gone to Macao, but with the embargo lifted, supplies were cheaper, and financial assistance more readily available in the other port, so Howel and Rowan agreed to bring the *Lady* on to Canton. She was brought through Macao up the Pearl river to Whampoa.

While Kendrick had excellent entrepreneuring ideas and was, in general, a solid seaman, he was rubbish when it came to figures. Poor Howel had his work cut out for him going through the paperwork to find out what was owed to whom. He couldn't go online and view an exact list of transactions— there were perhaps a few scribbled notes from Kendrick, and once creditors found out *Lady Washington* was there they arrived making demands; one of the main ways a creditor would receive payment during the time period was by being so irritating that the debtor couldn't take it any more and found the money. Howel also had to arrange selling the cargo late in the season, and received only 16,876 dollars for the pelts, seventy dollars for pearls, and 650 dollars for Kendrick's personal effects. After months of work, the supercargo managed to deduce that Kendrick and the brigantine were approximately 28,000 dollars in debt. That left almost 15,000 dollars still to pay off, not to mention the fact that she needed to be supplied and refitted for another voyage on the coast.

Howel was not happy about it, and wrote a long-winded complaint to Joseph Barrell about having been stuck with the problem. Her temporary commander James Rowan wisely shipped out on a different vessel, so Howel was on his own in Canton trying to work out what to do. Eventually he chose a similar course to Kendrick—and purchased *Lady Washington*. He paid the money up front and sold the brigantine to himself for 1,300 dollars. He told Barrell and the financiers that they really didn't want the massive debt and he was doing them a favor, which was in fact true.

Now that he had a vessel, Howel decided to officially go into the shipping business. He began a brokerage agency and went ashore where accommodations were more comfortable. Howel was extremely thorough, checking to make sure Kendrick's land deeds were properly filed with a notary and plenty of copies made. Since the Chinese and Portuguese were much more demanding with their debts than Captain Douglas and Martinez, Howel chose to pay them first, and basically ignored the Englishman and Spaniard's claims. He couldn't reimburse them when he had nothing to give, so he found a captain for the next season—Roger Simpson.

The *Lady* sailed under Captain Simpson as of 1795. Simpson is described as being an Englishman who comported himself as a gentleman and tended to be amiable and helpful to those he came into contact with; in general, he was a pleasant sort of fellow. The brig set out from Canton in July, but struck a, "dreadful typhoon...which blew away... sails," (Roe 135) and caused considerable damage. The wind always seemed to be coming from the wrong direction, and food ran short. As a result, Captain Simpson decided to go to Hawaii and wait until the next season to continue on to the Northwest coast. The crew weren't about to object to a balmy winter in the islands, so she sat snugly in Hawaii as other ships came and went. There were occasional storms during the night, but each morning, "many canoes thronged off from the shore

with vegetables...few hogs, and for those, nothing but powder
was demanded, and a middle sized hog could not be got
under a quart of that article," (Roe 135). The Hawaiians were
ruthless in their requests for guns and ammunition in return
for trade goods—unlike the natives of the Northwest coast
who accepted copper and other metals.

In January of 1796, Captain Broughton of the British ship
Providence arrived and was excellent company. The next
month, Captain Charles Bishop on board *Ruby* sailed into
the bay after a winter on the Northwest coast. He was
plagued by a leaky ship and disgruntled, freezing crew.
Bishop arrived in Waikiki on Saturday, February twentieth.
Lady Washington promptly sent an officer over to make
sure the new arrival had everything they needed, and
upon hearing that Bishop was desperately short of fresh
provisions, Captain Simpson sent over some vegetables
which were gratefully received.

The *Lady*'s captain went in person later that day and was
rendered full honours. The commanders mostly discussed
the fur trade, and Bishop decided it would be safer to ask
Broughton, commander of *Providence*, if the two of them
could sail in company to the dangerous coast. Broughton
was anchored at a nearby Hawaiian island, so *Ruby* resolved
to leave, especially after Simpson explained that there was
not that much meat to be had on the islands and everything
there was too expensive to trade for. When the poor *Ruby*

sprang a specially large leak, "through which water gushed in very fast," (Roe 137), Captain Simpson took *Lady Washington* to accompany them in the hunt for *Providence*, in case something serious went wrong and *Ruby* needed immediate assistance. The two vessels set off, giving three cheers for the Hawaiian chief on shore, who returned the honour enthusiastically. After several days, the *Lady* and her companion reached Waimea Bay on the twenty-third. Unfortunately, they found that *Providence* had sailed only the day before for the Northwest coast. Captain Bishop was severely disappointed, and quite worried about the state of his ship. The *Ruby* needed to be careened ashore, and Bishop did not trust the natives. It was also equally dangerous for him to set out for the coast with his vessel in such disrepair. Most of his crew were near desertion and did not want to get back on board and head for more freezing months along the Oregon and Washington coasts.

In the meantime, *Lady Washington* took advantage of the situation to do a series of trades for various supplies, and on the twenty-sixth of February, the *Lady*'s anchor stock broke. (This is the bar above the shank and below the ring.) Captain Simpson asked *Ruby*'s men to help, and they managed to replace it. The two captains became good friends—Simpson even wrote some letters of introduction to influential people in Canton and Macao, and Bishop agreed to take a bill back to Howel for his new friend. After a few last minute exchanges of supplies, as well as bundles of letters, three cheers were exchanged, and the *Ruby* set sail for China where she could properly refit. Captain Simpson decided to take the *Lady* on to the Northwest coast. A year later—by early 1797, the brig had successfully returned to Canton.

In March, Captain Bishop got rid of *Ruby*, with the help of Howel, and procured a better ship—*Nautilus*. Bishop realized that his previous season on the coast hadn't worked out well, so he requested that Roger Simpson join him on the new ship and sail in *Nautilus* to the Northwest coast. The two of them had got on well, so after a few months, Simpson and Bishop set out. The *Lady* was without a captain once again, and this time John Howel decided to try his own hand at commanding the *Lady*. Though Howel may have spent time on board the brig, he was lacking in practical command experience and training as a sailor, which proved disastrous.

On a visit to Macao, Howel came across young Daniel Paine. The two were fairly similar—highly intelligent men who chafed at ordinary life. Paine's family were ship builders, but he had not been interested in sitting about by the docks. At twenty-four years of age, Paine headed for New South Wales in Australia. A passionate revolutionary at heart, he fell in with a group who thought America's success in obtaining independence could also be true of Australia with the proper planning. Though Paine never did anything openly violent, and kept his support on a purely intellectual level, the British government began moving against the group and Paine wisely got on the next ship headed as far away as possible, which is how he found himself in China. Since Howel knew he would have his hands full as commander of *Lady Washington*, he wanted a supercargo who was trustworthy. Paine wanted to try living in India, since he was finding Macao a bit expensive, so Howel suggested that he come aboard *Lady Washington* until Manila, then find another ship from there to continue passage to India, and the young man agreed.

According to historians, China was running low on rice in the 1790s, and encouraged the cargo by lowering or even lifting tariffs entirely on ships carrying it. The nearest good source of rice was Manila in the Philippines. A ship brought extra ballast stones, sold them on the islands for construction of churches, then picked up a cargo of rice to sell back in Canton. A historian at the Maritime Museum in Hong Kong propounded that Howel indeed had a cargo of rice in mind when he sailed for Manila.

On the fourth of July, 1797, the brigantine up anchored and set out in stiflingly hot weather. The heat wave continued for days, until there was a brief rainstorm that was extremely welcome to the sweating crew. The brigantine continued south and began hitting major squalls, "fresh gales...thick weather with heavy showers of rain" (Frost 57). They had to be careful, due to strong currents, and Howel made a few mistakes in calculations as a result. *Lady Washington*

121

arrived at Lagayen Gulf in the Philippines, near Bolinao, on the thirteenth. She was forced to make a series of tacks during the night to maintain her distance from shore. The next day a local pilot was brought on board, but after sailing about for a while, no suitable anchorage was found until late in the afternoon. After the pilot returned ashore, the first officer got a notion into his head that they could find better anchorage on their own. For some reason Howel agreed, and they fiddled about for a while before giving up for the night.

The only civilization nearby was composed of a few bamboo huts off the ground, and the inhabitants were a curious mix of the native culture mingled in with Spanish and Chinese, rather like Joss Whedon's *Firefly*. Paine describes them in his journal as speaking a sort of random mix of different bits of languages, and dressing in rather a Chinese way, save for their hair and jewelry. On the sixteenth, a heavy squall blew up, turning even the protected bay into heaving seas. Despite the danger, a launch with six of the hands managed to come aboard that evening from visiting the brig's next destination—Caoayan. The *Lady* rocked so violently at anchor the next few days that Daniel Paine became dreadfully seasick and miserably clambered into his hammock until the weather calmed.

On the nineteenth, Howel hauled up one of the anchors, only to find the line had been worn through by constant rubbing on the rocks—he had not bothered to check it while they were moored and therefore lost the anchor. Frantically, he ordered the other hove up as well and discovered that they had saved it just in time, for the line was already fraying. A bit horrified at how close they had come to disaster, Howel decided it was best to move to a different and safer location. At nine o'clock in the morning, *Lady Washington* set out for Abra Canyon. The sailing launch trailed about a mile behind with a few of the crew, since she could not keep up with the brigantine. They expected to be reunited later.

On the twenty-first of July, early in the morning, *Lady Washington* attempted to enter the entrance of a river on her way to Caoayan. A native pilot had explained there was at least twelve feet of water above the bar, which meant there would be two feet of water under *Lady Washington*. Howel ought to have checked before sailing over it. Standard procedure involved taking careful soundings from a small boat—but there wasn't one on board. Their longboat had been stolen by some natives a few days before, and the launch wouldn't catch up for a while. Rather than waiting around, Howel sent the brigantine right at the bar, praying the pilot had been correct.

He was not—even during the rainy season the bar only had five or six feet of water over it. *Lady Washington* struck hard sand just as the weather began turning violent. It was a similar situation to when she had been in Tillamook, only the tide would not be enough to lift her free, and she could not kedge. Normally, a small boat with an anchor would be sent out, the anchor dropped, and the ship hauled clear. Only this time, the *Lady* had no small boat and no extra anchor. All Howel could do was set all her canvas and hope the force of wind would blow her clear. Paine believed some of the bad decisions were the result of the first mate being drunk at the time, and Howel no doubt relied heavily on the experience of a proper seaman. Other theories include the possibility that Howel enjoyed micromanaging and overruled the mate to bring the *Lady* over the bar. No matter how it occurred, she was stuck—a victim of owners trying to play sailor.

After five hours of the *Lady* being battered against the bar, the launch finally arrived. In the heavy sea it was difficult to get the anchor and hawser aboard the small boat, but it was finally managed. She sailed out, dropped the anchor and the *Lady* was hauled partway off, but stuck fast again. Some Philippine natives took their boats out to offer help, but there wasn't much they could do without having a second anchor. The tide and swells increased, so the first officer began trying to lighten the brigantine.

He offloaded the guns into the launch with orders to drop them close the shore and come back for more. Any heavy supply chests were put into the native boats, and Howel sent his own belongings, the medical supplies, and two men who were ill ashore as well. As the weather became worse, it was more difficult for small craft to reach the *Lady*, and the launch barely managed a return trip. There was nothing to be done save evacuate and hope *Lady Washington* was still there when the weather cleared, because huge waves beat not only against the brigantine but the shore—they had to get off before it was no longer possible. The first mate began loading everything of importance into the waiting boats—chests, bedding, supplies, and crew. Daniel Paine described his own experience trying to escape the brigantine, "after getting completely wet with the surf and a passage of near an hour...the boats continued with great difficulty to pass to and from the ship during the night," (Frost 60).

Evacuation continued into the next day as rain pelted the crew. By three o'clock in the afternoon of the twenty-second, all hands were ashore except for the mate and Portuguese cook who was too frightened to leave the ship. Everyone was wet through, and Daniel Paine caught a bad cold—their only shelter on shore was a rickety bamboo building that the wind whipped right through. They tried stuffing canvas against the slats, to little effect.

The exhausted first officer tried his best to get as much as he could on shore before finally leaving himself on the morning of the twenty-third. No more boats would dare venture near the *Lady*, so the mate had no choice but to jump into the frothing water. He called for the steward to join him, but to no avail. Shivering and clutching onto a halyard, the cook could not face a leap into the raging sea, despite the first mate's shouting pleas. He was already weakened from illness and preferred to stay on board what was left of the brigantine, hoping the storm would pass and he could get ashore safely. His decision proved fatal, for the Portuguese cook perished with the *Lady*.

The first mate had saved his own belongings for last, and tried to swim ashore with extra clothes, but lost them in the heavy surf. He staggered to shore around six o'clock in the morning and collapsed onto the sand. Misery continued as the storm showed no signs of abating for days—the sick men in the hut suffered in the cold with only bare necessities and no fresh provisions. Captain Howel set off to nearby Vigan to procure proper housing and relief.

Daniel Paine, though running a high fever, was the only one left by the river with the education to attempt medical treatments. He read through a book left in the medicine chest and did the best he could with what was on hand. The weather slowly calmed, and by the twenty-fifth of July, 1797, the sun began peeping out through the clouds. By evening it had turned warmer and almost pleasant with a light cloud cover. Captain Howel sent word that he'd found assistance and a house in Vigan. The next day what remained of *Lady Washington*'s crew, supplies, and guns set out for Vigan, leaving the wreck of the brigantine to perish. She was smashed badly and lay neglected—anything left that was valuable was taken by the locals and put to good use right down to her ballast. Most likely you could have seen what was left of her hull for the next few years and possibly even into the early 1800s, but eventually time eroded even her memory.

Lady Washington was the first American vessel to sail around Cape Horn and make a landing on the Northwest coast. She was the first to arrive in Japan, and among the earliest merchant vessels flying American colors to enter the world of international trade. From her indefatigable early years as a privateer fighting for the freedom of the colonies, to her adventures along unexplored coasts, she represents what it meant to be American. Her commanders may have been flawed, but they were fearlessly ready to face privation and danger. There is much we can learn from the courage of the early bold Northwestmen and *Lady Washington* herself.

WORKS CITED

Adventures at Sea in the Great Age of Sail: Five Firsthand Narratives. Captain Elliot Snow, ed. New York: Dover Publications, 1986.

Bancroft, Hubert Howe. The Works of Hubert Howe Bancroft. Vol, 21. San Francisco: A.L. Bancroft & Co, 1882-90.

"Books of Common Prayer: 1662." Anglicans Online. 2009 <http://anglicansonline.org/resources/bcp.html>.

Frost, Alan, R.J.B. Knight, ed. The Journal of Daniel Paine 1794-1797. Sidney: Library of Australian History, 1983.

Hayes, Derek. Historical Atlas of the Pacific Northwest: Maps of Exploration and Discovery. Seattle: Sasquatch Books, 2000.

The Journal and Letters of Captain Charles Bishop on the North-west Coast of America, in the Pacific and in New South Wales: 1794-1799. Michael Roe, ed. Cambridge: Cambridge UP, 1967.

Miller, Nathan. Sea of Glory: The Continental Navy Fights for Independence, 1775-1783. New York: D. McKay 1974.

Morgan, William James, ed. Naval Documents of The American Revolution. Vol. 6. Washington: Naval History Division, 1972.

Nokes, Richard J. Columbia's River: The Voyages of Robert Gray, 1787-1793. Tacoma: Washington State Historical Society, 1991.

Cross, Francis E., Charles M. Parkin. Captain Gray in the Pacific Northwest: Captain Gray's Voyages of Discovery 1787-1793. Bend: Maverick Publications, 1987.

Patton, Robert Holbrook. Patriot Pirates: the privateer war for freedom and fortune in the American Revolution. New York: Random House, 2008.

Rawley, James A., Stephen D. Behrendt. The Transatlantic Slave Trade Revised Edition. Lincoln: Nebraska UP, 2005.

Scharf, John Thomas. History of Maryland from the Earliest Period to the Present Day: 1765-1812. Baltimore: J.B. Piet, 1879.

Voyages of the Columbia to the Northwest coast. Frederic W. Howay, ed. Portland: Oregon Historical Society, 1990.

Made in the USA
Charleston, SC
07 July 2013